THE FU
OF WAR
FOR THE SICK AND DEMENTED

MAT VANCE

outskirtspress

DENVER, COLORADO

The Funny Side of War
For the Sick and Demented
v3.0

Outskirts Press, Inc.
http://www.outskirtspress.com

ISBN: 978-1-4787-5570-8

Outskirts Press and the "OP" logo are trademarks belonging to Outskirts Press, Inc.

PRINTED IN THE UNITED STATES OF AMERICA

My Thanks

J.T. and Washington during OSUT. We never saw each other after graduation, which is a shame, but you guys stuck up for me when my back was turned. Drill Sergeant's Anderson and Rouse, who taught me violence of action and vigilance.

Angel Madera, little did you know that you were my mentor when it came to conducting myself during training and at the bars. There was a time to work my ass off and there was a time to have fun with the guys. P.Y. Finley, you watched over me when I was just a puppy until it was time to let me go to the line and be another dumbass scout that can't work a radio.

White platoon during the 15-month tour, there were times I think we wanted to hurt each other more than any insurgents, but we stuck together and did a lot of good things that I'll never forget. Chris Hall and J.B. Williams, you were the answer to my question as a young NCO, "Will I ever get soldiers that aren't fucking worthless?" You 2 were the best and I only hope I led you well enough to become even better as both soldiers and men. Tim Delaughter, I never once considered myself anything but a loyal subordinate to you. You showed me how to perfect the art of fighting the good fight. Rob Jones, you made me laugh more than anyone and kept me sane. Rolando Sanchez, we started off in basic together and you taught me how to be patient throughout my entire service.

Bob "The Hurricane", Matty "Mayhem" Luhr and Chris "Oblivious" Bullis, we made up the Four Horsemen of the Apocalypse and had nothing but "epic" times together. You guys saw me at my worst and picked me up off my ass. That's a bond that can't be broken by time or distance.

Glenn Newman, Justin BEAUREGARD Courtney, Charles Olson, Grant MIKAL Rogers, Noe Gonzalez, Daniel "Swanny" Swanson, Anthony Mitchum and Kevin Meany... you guys put up with more shit than any group I've known. My second deployment was mind numbing and you guys made it out. I was so excited to be a leader to all of you at some point and you made me so proud. Your loyalty in rough times is something I think of daily. It's been an absolute privilege watching all of you evolve into the great men you are today.

To my friends, coming home to you saved my life. To my family in Idaho and New York, thanks for always supporting me and always welcoming me to visit. That's something not everyone is blessed with.

To my number one fan, my sister Heather, you are always so strong and never hesitate to help me. You never lost your cool when I was flipping the fuck out. I love you.

To my hero in life, my Dad. As soon as I enlisted you became a friend and I'm thankful for that everyday. I love you. To my Mom above, your fight and the way you lived followed by your passing broke my heart, but set me free to push my own limits and see what I was made of. I love you.

Table of Contents

Prologue

Regardless of what branch you served in, if you were in combat arms then you experienced many days where you almost died. That takes a toll on all of us, especially in situations where we wonder, "How am I alive and so many others are dead." It is my deepest wish that these stories will spark a good memory and help all of us think of the moments we laughed in the middle of all that mess. After all, do you think our fallen brothers want us to dwell on their ending or instead, celebrate how they lived their lives?

This book will open a civilian's eyes on what the comical side of military life during a time of war is really like. You typically only hear about heroism and going thru hell, which of course happens often, but what about the time between the firefights? Why can't we turn negatives into positives? Even in a hellish scene, human nature's comical side can still come to full bloom.

In chronological order, these stories will show my evolution as an average guy straight out of college from basic training to deploying to life in garrison and then to becoming a civilian again. Several subjects are heavy in meaning, but talked about lightly. Such areas are PTSD, racial discrepancies, poor leadership, drugs, alcohol, bar fights, etc. Enjoy the show...

WARNO! Fun with Words

It was an unspoken rule in my family while growing up that it's perfectly acceptable to use vulgar language as long as you were passionate towards what you were talking about and didn't substitute the "f-bomb" for "the." I've heard people throw around words like "ignorant" towards people that cuss in a fit of passion and to that I strongly disagree. I believe it's in a person's environment or culture of the household that determines such language. It's ignorant to assume the way you speak is the only verbally pure way to communicate. If it's used properly I've learned that under high stress, such as a firefight when some soldiers freeze up, using foul language at a high volume gets people moving in the right direction pretty quickly. I've literally seen crudeness and vulgarity save lives.

The following is in no way a normal person's vocabulary nor do I use such language now as a civilian. However, it's a part of the vast culture that is the military. If you're in combat arms, you can't escape it and you can't be offended by it. It's not for the faint of heart. Instead, it's for people that can adapt to nasty situations. Enjoy the ugly duckling of rhetoric below that will transcend into an enlightening smile as you read. You'll probably even think about it the next time someone cuts you off in traffic or a teenybopper says "like" for hundredth time in a 30 second conversation. These are words and phrases I encountered in the military and some are used throughout this book.

SUBLIMINAL MESSAGES – THE GRUNT TO CIVILIAN TRANSLATION

"This is a fuckcluster." – Somebody better organize this real quick like.

"I'm about to smoke your balls off." – I'm about to make you do a lot of painful exercises.

"Hey! Fuckstain!" – You just got caught doing something you're not supposed to be doing.

"Just start killing yourself." – Do pushups.

"Beat your chest!" - Do more pushups.

"Getting smoked." – To be punished with strenuous exercises until you've achieved total body muscle failure.

"He was probably suckin' on his momma's titty 'til the day he went to basic." – That kid was seriously sheltered and has no clue how the world works (mentally weak).

"Well, fuck me in the goat ass." – To this day I don't have the slightest idea what this means or insinuates. Perhaps it's a "Fuck My Life" moment and you know you're going to lose.

"Guy" – The mother of all subliminal insults... Saying "hey guy" or "look at this guy" when someone walks up is like calling that someone an inferior life form not of the human species.

"Zonk" – Go hide.

"Charlie Mike" – Coincides with the letters C and M. We use this as code for Continue Mission. If we were on patrol and something bad happened, but we were able to keep going, we would call up "Charlie Mike" on the net, or radio. It's OK to fall as long as you can Charlie Mike!

"Monday run day!"

"But it's Tuesday, SGT."

"So it's not Friday?"

"No, SGT."

"Then it's Monday run day!"– It's going to be a long PT (Physical Training) session and somebody will vomit.

"MANstrating" - Even dudes have a "time of the month."

"Congradu-fuckin-lations" – You seem excited with your accomplishments, but guess what? Nobody cares.

"FNG" – Fucking New Guy

"Mahogany." – Yep, I was just daydreaming about a swimsuit model while I'm surrounded by dudes in the middle of a patrol and I have a hard-on while going commando. A bit awkward.

ATTENTION GETTERS

"Shut your cockholster!"- Stop talking.

"Go suck start a .50 cal." – Stop talking.

"Wash your mouth out with buckshot." – Stop talking

"Come here, you!" – I'm about to make you cry.

"You cunt bucket." – Go away.

"Go play in traffic." – Go away

"Get your dick beaters off those!" – Don't touch anything!

MOTIVATIONAL WORDS

"Get the sand out of your vagina." – Stop being a whiny bitch.

"Unfuck yourself!" – You suck at life.

"Slap yourself." – You're fired.

"Man the fuck up!" – Oh you're hurting? Welcome to the party, Sally.

"Tonight, we're going to have a religious experience!" – I'm going to smoke you 'til you start hallucinating.

"The walls will run with sweat." – You're getting smoked in a small room with no ventilation until condensation forms on the windows and cinderblock walls. Yes, it's possible.

BEST BRIEFS

Weekend briefs were by commanders to warn us to stay out of trouble over the weekend while in the States. Pre-mission briefs were given while deployed by the highest-ranking person in our platoon prior to going on a mission, detailing what to expect. Usually all were several minutes too long, except for these two.

BEST WEEKEND BRIEF ~ By Captain Bryan Hatcher
"Don't fry your bacon naked." – Think before you act... I think.

BEST PRE-MISSION BRIEF ~ By Captain Ryan Nystrom
"Don't die." – It's simple guys; just don't die while on this patrol in Baghdad at the height of this war. Easy, right?

You made it! And this is just the tip of the iceberg people, but you get the point. If you are offended, I do not apologize. These are verbatim phrases that I encountered on my adventures. While some are hurtful if they are directed at you, most of them are funny if they are directed elsewhere. Now, go motivate someone to unfuck themselves.

BASIC

While sitting on a curb outside my hotel in Richmond, VA prior to shipping out to basic training at Fort Knox, Kentucky in June of 2004 I tried to imagine what I was about to embark on. The sun was setting as my sister and dad said their goodbye's still not sure what to think of my decision to enlist during spring break of my senior year at Christopher Newport University in Newport News, VA. I just had to get the hell away from everyone and everything I knew and go on an adventure before the socially acceptable task of going to college and settling into a desk-ridden career choked the fucking life out of me.

Reception and the Marine with Jokes

Upon arriving at Fort Knox, I was placed in reception. Reception was the place everyone goes to while waiting for their number to be called to officially start basic; a holding facility, if you will. My number was 060 and it was at that moment that I realized I was just a number in the masses of soldiers our country has produced. I'd have to work hard to become more than just a number and statistic that the average American wouldn't give a damn about.

Reception was every man for himself and we had absolutely nothing to do except stand in formations for hours waiting for something to happen or for our number to be called. I remember being called to a formation at midnight and we got to see the sunrise together while some guys collapsed on their faces as they fell asleep standing up. How romantic. This went on for over a week. If we weren't in formation or in line for chow learning how to move "nut-to-butt," we would be in the barracks. People wouldn't hesitate to steal from one another. I wasn't surprised when I later found out how many men joined the military to avoid jail time. I found a couple of guys that could be trusted and we watched each other's backs.

One soldier, Nguyen, was a soft-spoken Vietnamese man who seemingly had a lot of pain in his past that he didn't want to reveal.

He looked like a smaller version of the Asian bad guy in all the 80's movies, especially the ones with Jean Claude Van Dam. It's always nice to have a diesel looking guy on your side. Nguyen left the barracks room one day and this guy, Crapp, started rummaging thru his locker. I yelled at Crapp to get out and hoped that we wouldn't have our numbers called to be in the same basic training platoon. I wasn't so lucky. He claimed he wasn't going to take anything. So why go into another person's locker? He could then add liar to his resume along with being a failed thief.

The other guy to watch my back was a marine named Reece. Reece was thin, light haired and confident in his knowledge of how the military worked. He could tell if someone was legitimately allowed to bark orders at us or not. Some guys at reception had been their longer and would yell at newer guys like myself to get out of the way or do push ups since they knew we'd listen to anyone with balls at that point. Reece protected us from that. My team was set and picking a good team was something I became very good at.

Reception was also a place where guys could decide to make a run for it or not. A lot of people got to reception and realized they made a huge mistake by enlisting or they were clean and sober enough to see they made a mistake and signed a contract. Reece came up to me in formation one day.

"Vance, did you hear about last night?" he asked.

"No, what happened?"

"Two dudes wanted to get out of their contract so they arranged to get caught blowing each other in the cleaning closet."

"Yeah right! That's too extreme, man, c'mon"

"Shhhhh!" an annoyed soldier-to-be hissed as we spoke in a formation where speaking wasn't allowed.

"Oh fuck off, ya narc. Nobody's going to check on us for hours," Reece said forcefully.

"Did you actually see it go down?" I asked

"No, but while I was on fire guard I definitely heard a drill screaming while dragging both of them off down the hall."

It was the summer of 2004, when 'Don't ask, don't tell' was still in full effect. I was shocked two heterosexuals would go that far though. Reece loved telling stories like that. He told me about the jokes his buddies in the marines played on each other. Reece told me that one of his buddies sent him a package with homoerotic messages on the box so when he went for mail call everyone would see the false evidence. I found this hilarious. I wish I found it a red flag when he asked for my address as I left for basic and he was stuck in reception for another week. Not my brightest moment. Eventually I was in basic and a drill summoned me down to the front desk of the barracks.

"If you want this mail, private, you gonna have to earn it," said the size large black drill with a Pepe Le Pew mustache and Louis Armstrong voice.

"Yes, drill sergeant," and the push-ups commenced.

"Private, is your name Vance?"

"Yes, drill sergeant."

"Get the fuck up."

I got back to my feet as the letter was mid-flight en route to the desk and the drill had already turned to walk away. It was as if he didn't want anything to do with the letter, nor me for that matter. I took that as a hint to grab my letter and go back to my platoon's floor. I looked down at the envelope and my face turned beet red. I grabbed the letter and left as I noticed the two privates standing close to the drill with his back still turned were working really hard not to laugh. The letter was from Reece and he was kind enough to put hearts with X's and O's all over the envelope with a return address from a mysterious man named, "Joe." The letter itself simply read, "Gotchya Vance! Reece" That son of a bitch.

The Drills, The Pit and The Pain

"All right privates! Put all of your gear back in your duffle bags and lock them up!" screamed Drill Sergeant Anderson after we were done checking our inventory.

"Drill sergeant, this lock won't fit on my duffle bag," I panicked, as my lock was too thick to fit in the metal loop to secure my duffle bag.

"Then you will **MAKE IT FIT**, private!"

"Yes, drill sergeant!"

I squeezed the tiniest portion of the lock that would fit in the metal loop and used every ounce of pathetic strength I had to produce torque and pried the loop wider. It worked! It was the first day of basic training and that crazy Drill Sergeant, or Drill, just Jedi-mind tricked my ass into bending metal. Was it really Jedi-mind tricks or the fact that the pressure he put on me forced me to stop being a little bitch?

Basic wasn't what I thought it would be. I imagined a world where these brutes wearing brown Canadian Mountie hats would beat the hell out of us for breathing in the wrong direction. Not so much. Drills were still a scary group of gents at first glance. They wore their Mountie hats at such a downward angle that they exposed the back of their heads and completely hid their eyes. Not being able to see a man's face makes him ninja-like and you know not to piss him off or you'd face some kind of numb chuck barrage. It didn't matter how tall, short, skinny or fat the drill was; if they made eye contact with someone from the shadows of that hat then that person knew they were in deep shit.

Drills weren't allowed to actually beat us, so they smoked us. To smoke someone was to make them do physical exercises until their muscles gave out, bled or puked all over themselves. It was a punishment used to teach quick lessons when soldiers messed up or to humiliate a soldier when they needed to be humbled. One such method was taking us to "The Pit." It consisted of a rectangular space on the ground roughly 30 feet across and 60 feet in length. The borders were made of ancient wooden 4 x 4's and the space in the middle was filled with sawdust. When sawdust is dry it kicks up into the air when you're doing "exercises" in the pit. This makes breathing very difficult and if you have cuts on your body it stings.

Drills became older brother figures, constantly putting us in our place. DS Anderson looked like the drill right out of the movie, "Full Metal Jacket," only he was shorter than most of us privates. Drills would often bump their chests on a private's chest as they barked to let them know how upset they were. This Neanderthal approach at showing us who the boss was didn't work for a short drill like Anderson. He had to repeatedly jump to bump chests with privates while barking at them. JT found this too funny to contain himself.

JT was a tall, skinny, white Kentucky boy with a southern draw and lots of confidence. He wasn't afraid of anything and he enjoyed living life to the fullest. JT was the guy that would take bets to eat certain critters and was going thru basic to be in the National Guard, or to be a Nasty Girl, as us active duty people called them. He just couldn't contain himself when DS Anderson was upset and jumping around.

"What the fuck are you laughing at private!" yelled Anderson.

"Nothing, Drill Sergeant!" JT yelled back while failing to keep a straight face.

"Beat your face, private!"

"Yes, Drill Sergeant!" JT started doing push-ups with a smile.

"Anybody else think I'm a fucking comedian?"

"No Drill Sergeant!" yelled the platoon as JT continued to fail at trying to display a poker face and the rest of us chuckled.

"Keep it up privates and tonight we're going to have a religious experience!"

Game over. We wanted no part in getting smoked inside the barracks. The pit was one thing since it was naturally built for pain, but inside the barracks is where the real evil creativity of a drill took place. One night we lined up in the hall with our backs to the wall. We were then told to lean forward and touch the other side of the narrow hallway. There was a catch. We had to hold ourselves off the wall with just one finger per hand while another private at the end duck walked under us. Religious experiences with drills were never heavenly.

I can only imagine that with each generation of drills, there was a magical book of pain passed on. It had ideas on how to "fix" privates and each drill would add another idea as his time came to move on. I was most impressed with how quickly a drill could turn such a lovely evening into a nightmare.

While on an FTX, or Field Training Exercise, I had to set up a dry place to sleep in the rain with my poncho. It was pitch black outside, but as scouts we were trained to have light and noise discipline. I failed at both disciplines that night and paid the price at the hands of DS Anderson. I pulled out a flashlight and loudly rummaged thru my gear. Out of nowhere, Anderson pops out of a fucking bush in the middle of the woods.

"Hand over that light, private," Anderson ordered.

I handed it to him and he immediately threw it 30 meters deeper into the woods, down a hill.

"Low crawl, go."

I just looked at him as if to say, "Where did you... what the hell, man?"

"10! 2! 1!" there was something seriously wrong with his count down, but it was like when a parent is angry at their child and tells them they have ten seconds to go to their room or there will be a serious ass whipping.

I was halfway thru some thorn bushes when Anderson got bored and told me to maintain light discipline and get some shuteye. Sweet. It was a quick and effective lesson as I felt blood running down the left side of my face from the thorns and an itch spanning my entire body from who knows what. The next day I woke up with chiggers buried into my left ankle and shin. A little Elmer's glue spread over the infected area cured the chigger issue and I never forgot about noise and light discipline again. So many lessons in a short amount of time!

Despite teaching us various forms of torture, DS Anderson was great to us. He wasn't fond of mass punishment like other drills. It was very rare that he took us to the pit or smoked us in the barracks. Other platoons seemed to be out there daily. We'd always sneak to the windows of the barracks to watch other platoons get smoked. It was a sick entertainment that we direly needed.

Our troop was Echo Troop. It consisted of four platoons. I was in fourth platoon on the third floor along with third platoon. They made several trips to the pit. One day two members of third platoon were caught with a large bag of candy inside the barracks, which was a major no-no. The two culprits were told to sit on the edge of the pit in nice comfortable chairs their drills sarcastically provided for them.

"Alright privates, we're going to have some fun until these two blue falcons finish their bags of candy!" their drill stated.

"Kuh-kaw! Kuh-kaw!" the platoon chirped back.

A blue falcon was essentially a buddy-fucker. If you did anything that got your boys in trouble or did something selfish, you were deemed a blue falcon and a bit of an outcast. Everyone knew the bag of candy contained way too much sugar for any two people to finish in one sitting. The smoke session commenced as the platoon was ordered to start low crawling from the opposite side of the comfortably sitting privates and move in their direction.

Low crawling consisted of a private lying on his stomach and one side of his face firmly planted on the ground, or sawdust in this case since they were in the pit. The only way to move forward was to use one arm and one leg to drag their own body. Low crawling was developed to move low to the ground while under fire or suspicion of an enemy presence. It's quite uncomfortable and slow moving, usually causing blood loss from multiple scrapes along the entire body from the terrain. About ten minutes into the smoke session, the two buddy-fuckers were puking their brains out.

"Ohhhh yeah, there we go privates! Made the blue falcons pop!" a drill laughed. "Now finish eating!"

"We can't, Drill Sergeant!" one of the blue falcons whimpered.

"Well sure ya can! You bought it so don't go wastin' it now!"

More barfing…

"Alright 3rd Platoon, recover and get inside!"

"Kuh-kaw! Kuh-kaw!"

"You two turds toss that bag of shit in the trash and get the fuck outta my sight!"

And yet another lesson learned.

Inserts

Another source of entertainment came from "inserts." Inserts were soldiers that were already in the military and wanted to re-class, or change jobs. In order to change jobs, they were inserted into the scout-training portion of OSUT, which was the 8 weeks after the initial 8 weeks of basic. Typically we received inserts that had previously been in POG positions. Pronounced "pogue," it meant "persons other than grunts." They were non-combat arms positions like pack clerk or finance. You'd think they could teach us a thing or two about the military, but the only thing they taught us was the word "roger." It sounded foreign to us, so we fought the transition from "Yes, drill sergeant" to "Roger, drill sergeant." Who the fuck is Roger?

When a POG deploys they always come back with "war stories." Chances are that if the story is coming from a POG, it's a bit exaggerated. Third platoon got a parachute rigger, PR, as an insert and this guy was an asshole. He was in his late-30's, gray, wrinkly, always angry and obviously didn't age well. PR thought that his Staff Sergeant E-6 rank gave him pull around a bunch of privates. The inserts just didn't understand that everyone in OSUT was the same rank. My college degree made me a Specialist E-4 rank, but I sure as hell knew that was worthless during OSUT. Ole gimpy, crusty PR was annoying the drills one day so they set him up for failure and got his ass good. A 17-year old private was popping his mouth off to PR.

"You just gonna to take that?" asked the drills.

The drills egged him on knowing full well that an insert was not supposed to smoke a private. The private happened to be one of the candy vomiters, so it was easy for PR to assume it was acceptable to smoke him. PR took him to the pit and started him off with lunges then rolling left and right and then moved on to low crawling. While this was going on the drills saw Sergeant Major Beurns walking up and quickly dispersed into the barracks as if they were us after we saw a drill coming. Everyone answers to somebody. A Sergeant Major is the highest rank on the enlisted side of the military.

SGM Beurns was a bad ass. He was a tall, bald, well-built, formidable individual with a voice that shook even the drills to their bones. Beurns' sole purpose was to enforce rules and regulations on everyone lower ranking than him. He curiously walked up from behind PR, which gave PR no chance to react. Beurns quietly stood beside him, as he was enjoying the smoke session. We all watched from the barracks' windows in awe. Sucks to be PR.

"Hey there staff sergeant," Beurns calmly said.

PR took one look at the rank and stood accordingly.

"Sergeant Major," PR said nervously.

"Hey private, go away."

"Yes, Sergeant Major!" yelled the mouthy private.

Beurns waited to be alone with PR. We could see a horrified look on PR's face, as he knew he was in deep shit despite Beurns being so calm. Then our entertainment commenced. Our faces were like a guy bragging to his buddies that he just scored a hot chick's number.

"Get the fuck down! Roll right! Roll left!" ordered Beurns.

He explained to PR how he "appreciated" his enthusiasm, but also let PR know he was on the same level as the rest of us. PR was told to never attempt to smoke any of us again. It was like watching a high school bully get beaten to a pulp by a WWE superstar. Beurns took a quick glance up at the barracks' windows and we all hit the floor. The show was over, but the damage was done. PR finished OSUT like an abused dog following its master with his head down.

Beurns taught me something unique about punishment that day. He had to smoke PR, but with PR's experience and rank he didn't want to do it in front of anyone out of respect of PR's service. Beurns made PR think he was protecting him from humiliation, yet Beurns knew we were watching. He did all of this on purpose and glared at us as if to say, "It's wrong that you're watching right now, but this one's for you guys." His glare came with a smirk. Beurns knew PR was a dirt bag that deserved what he got, but it wasn't the proper way to punish an E-6. That glare he gave us taught me to pick and choose carefully how I punish a soldier. Humiliation humbles and there is a time and a place for it, but there is also a time for fake subtlety.

Potato Soap and Aliens

Sleep depravation over a long period of time causes stress. Stress causes people to snap or just start acting loopy. Basic Training was my first encounter with such conditions and two of my bunkmates did just that. Washington was one and Wilde was the other. Wilde was a simple man. He was a tall, husky white boy from some po-dunk Pennsylvania town. Drill Sergeant Rouse asked him why he joined the military one afternoon.

"To get revenge for my friend that was killed in Iraq, drill sergeant," was Wilde's response.

"If he thinks he's going to find the people that killed his friend, then he's a fuckin' idiot," DS Rouse said. "This isn't WWII where the enemy wears a uniform and you just kill as many as you can."

Wilde definitely thought it was that type of war. It seems that calling him a simple man was a generous description. Echo Troop went out to train one night and our mission was to hold our defensive position. Wilde was put in charge of our platoon on a hilltop and I suspect it was purely for the drill's entertainment. The drills organized a team to harass us all night so we couldn't sleep and to see how we'd react under that kind of stress. Well, ole Wilde saw one of the enemy forces sneak up and instead of staying together at an easily defensible position in the high ground, he took off thinking we'd follow. He thought wrong.

"I see 'em! I see 'em! *Charge!*" he screeched.

Charge? Really dude? Are we training for the fuckin' Civil War now? How about the American Revolution? Good luck with the Redcoats buddy. Wilde was dispatched by a volley of blanks from the enemy and wasn't allowed to call the shots anymore after that night.

That battle cry wouldn't be his only moment of splendor. Wilde had a habit of sleep walking and talking. He would be my first encounter with someone that did that and it was memorable. Basic sure provided a lot of firsts for me. When Wilde would start mumbling in his sleep, the rest of us in the room would try to get a conversation out of him, but usually to no avail. One night we got something even better than a conversation; we got to see a freaked out drill having a colorful conversation with Wilde instead.

I woke in the middle of the night to see Wilde standing at attention against the wall between two bunks with his eyes closed. To animate how scary it looked, Washington had his green, L-shaped Vietnam era flashlight shining on Wilde's face by the time I woke. Wilde looked liked the crazy private from "Full Metal Jacket."

"Wilde are you ok?" I asked.

"Potato soap!" he yelled at the top of his lungs.

"You mean potato soup?"

"Soap! Potato soap!"

We laughed our asses off and then a drill walked in.

"Private Wilde, what the fuck are you doing?" questioned the heavy set, black, high-pitched, fast-talking third platoon drill.

"Potato soap, drill sergeant!"

"Wilde, are you fuckin' with me?"

"Potato soap!"

"It's lights out now get the fuck to bed!"

"Yes, drill sergeant!"

Wilde actually walked straight to bed with his eyes still closed as the drill walked away. He didn't lie down though. Wilde moved his military issued green blanket and top white sheet to the side as if he was going to lie down. Instead, he sat Indian-style facing the pillow's end of the bunk. Sitting up straight with his eyes closed he started to moan and mumble as usual. Then he started opening his eyes and looked confused.

"You there, Wilde?" asked Washington.

"Yeah?"

"You know a drill just came in here and yelled at ya, right?

"No. Am I in trouble?"

"Naw, but that drill probably thinks you crazy now."

"Shit."

Stress affects people in different ways. Washington had a few moments of his own where he just acted loopy as hell. Our platoon was standing in formation after another long day at the range. DS Rouse came up to us and started to give commands to start marching. He was still new at being a drill and giving commands wasn't his strong suit. When somebody makes a mistake while giving commands in the military, that soldier can correct himself by saying "as you were" to the formation he is talking to in order to back his formation up to their previous stance. This allows the formation to not be confused, take a step back and everyone gets on the same page. It is not something a private should say to a drill. You're safer walking up to a bull with a red jumpsuit and sending a backhand right across the snout.

"Atten-huh!" Rouse said, sounding like he knew he already messed up.

"As you were drill sergeant!" yelled Washington.

"Who the fuck said that!" DS Anderson stepped in to defend a fellow drill.

"I did, drill sergeant!"

Anderson made a b-line for Washington, bulldozing past anyone in his path to justice. He started jumping up in the air so his chest could bump the chest of the much taller statured private. We often wondered what would happen if he and Wilde ever pissed each other off. Maybe it would have been a reenactment of the famous bathroom scene in "Full Metal Jacket." Nah, we liked Anderson too much to hope for that. If you pissed him off he would go right up to you and jump into your chest for intimidation purposes.

"You don't *ever* correct a drill! Why the *fuck* are you talking in formation?"

"He didn't address us drill sergeant!"

"Shut the *fuck* up, private! Get over there in the grass!"

Rouse was supposed to stand at attention and then say, "Platoon, attention!" A minor detail that only Washington picked up. Washington was a tall, strong black guy that I became very good friends with. He did JROTC in high school and had a heart of gold. Washington was a good leader bound to do great things in his military career. When he was our platoon guy, or leader, he would stay up until two or three in the morning mopping the floors so they would look fresh for the drills and the rest of us could sleep peacefully. Unfortunately, he didn't know that drills don't like to be corrected by the very people they are teaching.

"I'm about to start calling you guys the "Window Licker" platoon, since you want to act like you ride the short bus," Rouse said. "In fact, when I call you to attention I want you all to sound off like the bunch of retards you're acting like!" We literally had to go, *"errrrrr!"*

Rouse could say all he wanted. Washington was our hero that day. Not a single one of us had the balls to do what he did. It was just a shame that Anderson was smoking him while we marched off and he would have to run to catch up after "learning his place." Washington didn't do what he did to be a smart ass or a Mr. Know-It-All. He did it because it was instinctual. Washington actually had a confused look on his face while he was being smoked as if to say, "Why am I being punished?" He was just loopy like that. It wouldn't be the last time he did something out of the blue to make us all love him. Our platoon was getting ready for lights out when Washington was looking at all of our beds in the leadership room.

"Guys, I want something new. Lets move our beds around," he said.

"I don't think this is the best place to redecorate, man," I said.

Washington went ahead and moved his bed perpendicular to the rest of our beds so one long side was flat against the wall. He was so happy that he was able to make a simple change, but the rest of us just laughed. We knew the drill on duty that night would walk by and not approve.

Lights out. I could here the footsteps. Here we go. It was hard not to laugh as the drill's footsteps came to a complete stop at our doorway and we could just feel his body temperature rise as his heart rate peaked and his gigantic eyes tried to escape his head. I just rolled over and covered my head.

"Washington! What the fuck did you do to your bunk!" said the same poor drill that walked in on Wilde's "potato soap."

"What do you mean, drill sergeant?" Washington played dumb.

"Private, how the *fuck* did your *bunk* get against the wall like that?"

"Aliens. Aliens must have done it, drill sergeant."

I rolled back over to see the massacre. Washington was just sitting on his bed with the most innocent look on his face.

"Why is it always somebody in this room that's fuckin' wit me? Get to fuckin' bed, privates!"

"Yes, drill sergeant," we all said together as the drill walked off.

We all turned our attention back to Washington and looked at him in awe.

"What?" Washington enquired, now with a smile added to his

innocent face.

"How are you not in the pit getting smoked right now?" I asked.

"Aliens."

We started laughing yet again.

"Get tah fuckin' sleep, privates!" yelled the drill from down the hall.

I have a feeling when the drills saw things like that they had to walk away so we didn't see them laughing. Memories like this one make the hard days in life a little easier. It's something I'd always come across when I'd least expect it and will always appreciate.

Bored^2 + Curious^2 = Stupid^2

"That's the biggest, hairiest, most colorful caterpillar we could find," Washington said.

"Alright, get the pot up to 50 bucks and I'll eat it," JT promised.

"All we got is 15."

"Close enough."

A few of us had finished our land navigation early and decided to gather at the top of a moss-covered hill near Fort Knox to hide from those scary drills. JT grabbed the juicy critter and held it in suspense over his mouth as his head tilted back. Basic training drove us to such extremes to pass time between smoke sessions with the drills.

"No, no, no! Oh shit, ew, ew, ewwww!" we all gasped.

JT smiled, chewed and swallowed what hoped to become a butterfly, but those dreams were cut short thanks to a bunch of bored privates. This boredom killer of a ritual didn't stop in basic. It would follow me throughout my entire time in the military. The only difference was that as privates became soldiers, money didn't have to be the great motivator. Back in basic though, a few bucks would send us laughing into the night.

I'll always say that I never met a dirt bag until I joined the military. One in particular was a plus sized Puerto Rican named Soar-ass. He had a hilarious lisp when he spoke. Now to his credit, he could somehow move his jellyroll-looking body real fast, but besides that he was only good for comic relief for the rest of us. Soar-ass was going thru OSUT to be a Nasty Girl and I'll never forget the day our drills told him that his unit was activated to deploy and he would join them as soon as he graduated.

"Soar-ass! Your Pennsylvania unit has been activated!" yelled a drill.

"Like, what do you mean, drill sergeant?" he whined.

"It means you are going to deploy, buttercup!"

"Yes, drill sergeant," and the panic set in.

Soar-ass didn't join the military to deploy, which made us all very curious as to why he would enlist in combat arms during a time that our country was in two different wars.

"Guys I don't want to go!"

"Then why are you here?" we questioned.

"To look good in uniform an' make my family proud."

Yet another moment that everyone's jaws dropped. To look good in uniform. You have to be fucking kidding me. That was his mentality throughout OSUT; to just do the bare minimum to get that uniform. We didn't like Soar-ass much after that, so there was one night we got him to do something incredibly stupid. I was in my room getting ready for lights out when I heard an awful scream from down the hall.

"Ow, ow, ow, ow, ow!" screamed Soar-ass as he ran down the hall and into the cleaning closet across the hall from my room.

"What was that all about?" I asked my bunkmates.

I didn't get an answer so we piled into the hallway to look into the closet only to see Soar-ass spread eagle with his pants down and the sink turned on full blast, aimed at his crotch. After the pain settled he looked up and realized we were all staring.

"I put Icy-Hot on my balls," he moaned.

The entire 44 man-platoon erupted into laughter. I couldn't sleep too well after that. Sleep was something that just didn't happen much during OSUT due to the training schedule or guys putting spicy cream on their nut sack making me giggle all damn night. You have to laugh at the little things.

Holla Back Girl

We rarely had an opportunity to make phone calls. When we did, we would only have three minutes to spit out as much as we could and then abruptly hang up. One day we were walking in formation en route to the short row of three phone booths behind the barracks. There were two unfamiliar privates already there. This displeased DS Anderson, but drills wouldn't mess with privates they didn't know, unless those privates happened to be tankers. Tankers were in training to be on a big ass Abrams A-1 tank. They had their own area they had to stay in, but their drills were a lot more lenient than ours. On top of that, the first time we were allowed to go to the post store for toiletries we ran into some tankers. They were bragging about some type of simulator where they drove behind scouts on the ground that were calling in an attack.

"Yeah man, I only killed 19 scouts today!" one fat tanker said to another.

"Did he just say what I think he said?" I asked.

"That's bull shit, man," said JT

I guess tankers ran over or shot scouts while driving behind us in the simulator. Not comforting words of confidence and it didn't help that they were laughing about it. This left a bad taste in all of our mouths regarding tankers. However, DS Anderson eased our troubled minds that day at the phone booths.

"Are you two turds scouts?" asked Anderson.

"No," said one tanker.

"No? No *what* motherfucker!"

"No, drill sergeant," they quivered and stood proper.

"Start pushing! Well, what the fuck are you doing here?"

"Using the phone, drill sergeant."

"No the fuck you're not. You're in scout territory and these are phones for scouts only. You know, *real* fuckin' men!"

Anderson smoked the tankers for a couple of minutes and then sent them running. It was great to see a drill say something nice about his platoon, no matter how mundane. It's a small relief to see them do that for you after months of riding your ass. It didn't take long to go back to normal though. Anderson then smoked everyone that was done with the phone to put pressure on everyone else to hurry up. He didn't give us much time to enjoy him picking on someone other than us. It was just his style and a style that I would take with me in life.

Anderson always took time to laugh at the simple things, even if it started out with him being extremely pissed off. Our platoon was at the range one day and learned the importance of the proper form of range walking. We were apparently moving too slow throughout a range so upon our return to the barracks, Anderson explained that when a drill screamed "range walk!" you were to walk as fast as humanly possible without actually picking up a jog. This safely ensures that time at the range will be at a minimum, which is always nice when working with a platoon full of people that have no idea what they're doing. I've always had respect for positions like drills or teachers. They get a group of morons, teach them how not to be morons and then get a whole new batch of morons. I would go nuts in their shoes, or boots.

We all went behind the barracks fearful that Anderson was going to take us to the pit, but instead he smiled and told us to line up in two rows behind him.

"All right, privates! Since you mouth breathers don't know how to move with a purpose, we're going to range walk until I believe you understand. Think of it as a race. First two, go!" he barked.

Off we went, two at a time to the end of the sidewalk, which was 200 feet away. The losing line would be rewarded with push-ups of course. As we were racing we had to wear our pistol belts. The funny thing about pistol belts is that our belts didn't have any pistols. Instead they only carried two canteens, one on each hip. Walking as fast as you can with two canteens highlighting your hip movement provided a lot of entertainment we didn't see coming.

It came time for the smallest guy in our platoon to race. Coincidently he had to race one of the tallest guys. Wilson was white, had light brown hair, stood 5'6" and weighed maybe 135 lbs soaking wet. He spoke quietly with a thick Tennessee accent, wore thick, brown-framed military glasses half the size of his face and listened to heavy metal music. Not the most threatening looking or sounding individuals, but if you crossed him he would come at you with everything he had. Wilson would always admit when he was scared, but never once acted like it. It's a mentality we both shared and brought us close as friends.

Wilson took off with the mission of winning. We all new this wasn't going to happen, but for some reason we all went ape-shit cheering for him. The race was out of reach for him to win, but that didn't stop him from trying his best. Wilson was in full angry granny walking mode with his hips swinging violently side-to-side. This action combined with everyone going nuts even brought Drill Sergeants Anderson and Rouse to tears laughing and applauding Wilson's effort.

"Atta girl, Wilson! You sexy lady you!" yelled Anderson.

"Fuck *yew geyes!*" Wilson yelled back while smiling at all of us.

We were all stressed out and needed a laugh. Something that simple made us smile all the way thru lights out that night and into morning formation the next day.

Ritalin

One of the rare times I was smoked as an individual was due to an investigation. An investigation as to who had chewing tobacco. I know, how trifling. No one was allowed to chew or smoke tobacco during basic. Even the drills weren't supposed to smoke, chew or drink around the privates, so you know damn well they were always in a pissy mood and if they couldn't do it, we'd be punished harshly for such acts. On a side note, one of the drills still managed to fill his camelback with whiskey for every march we did. We got a buzz just smelling it come out of his pores.

The person in question during this investigation was someone I became good pals with, JT. One thing JT missed just as much as his girlfriend during basic was chewing tobacco. Somehow he had it smuggled in and had gotten away with it for a couple of months, but he messed up and a drill found a dip can hidden in the bathroom, or latrine, excuse my French. Learning military dialect was always hilarious to me.

The drill was furious that one of his privates was enjoying something that he could not openly do. We were headed to the pit. Unfortunately for our drills, we were a tight nit platoon and not so eager to rat on a good man. Unfortunately for JT there would eventually be a rat and it would be one of his own bunkmates.

I was in the leadership room with only four others. Typically if any of us messed up, we would be replaced. We made it thru most of the 16 weeks of training together, which is unheard of. JT was one of those leaders. The rat in the house, Ritalin, was another. Ritalin was only in that room because he was good with computer programs the drills used to keep all the private's training and progress in order. Ritalin had dark brown hair and freckles peppered his cheeks. He was of average height, thin, completely nonathletic and annoyingly hyper. The kid was also a pathological liar.

Ritalin knew we couldn't prove anything he said during basic, so he filled us with a lot of BS. He told us his great, great grandfather was the first recipient of the Medal of Honor during the Civil War and that his brother had recently earned one in Iraq as a scout. Ritalin said his brother was killed while earning the medal, so of course none of us contested his proud claims. After basic I regained access to the Internet and did some research. That lying motherfucker. He also claimed that he was higher ranking than all of us, because he had done college courses and JROTC during high school. The rank was definitely a lie too; only it was a drill that called him out in front of everyone.

"That's not the way it works, private, so shut the fuck up!" yelled DS Rouse.

If our eyes represented applause, that drill got the longest call for an encore in the history of mankind that day. Ritalin was bitter about that and he looked to vent any way he could. It was only a matter of time before a weakling like that would crack under pressure. In the pit we began to sweat and gasp for air all in the name of tobacco.

"Whoever did it just fess up and stop being a blue falcon," cried Ritalin.

"Shut the fuck up, private!" all the drills despised that little shit bird.

Rouse realized the pit wasn't working and sent us into the

barracks to stand by for another smoke session. As he was plotting our torturous night to come, the platoon's leaders gathered.

"Vance, I'm just going to call it," JT told me.

"Yeah, you should admit it you fucking buddy fucker!" Ritalin screeched.

"Just for that outburst, let it ride, JT," I suggested while glaring at Ritalin, "as far as Rouse knows, that dip can has been in the latrine since the last cycle of privates."

Ritalin looked like he was going to cry. A drill walked into our room first.

"I'm going to make the walls wet with your sweat if I don't get answers, privates."

I could immediately tell he was bluffing and about to just smoke us for a few minutes then call it a night. Ritalin wasn't so good at reading people.

"I know who did it, drill sergeant," Rouse turned to Ritalin and he about crapped his pants, "well, I mean, I know that Vance knows who did it, drill sergeant."

"The *fuck* I do Ritalin," I denied.

"Watch your fuckin' mouth, Vance," Anderson jumped in, "Well, who did it?"

"Drill sergeant, I do not know who did it."

"Yeah you do Vance, just say it," yet another weak, whiny cry from Ritalin that made me think of the part from the Never-Ending Story where the girl keeps saying, "Say my name Atreyu, just say my naaaaaaame." You know what I'm talking about, '80's babies!

"No I do not."

"Step into my office, Vance," said Anderson with a calmer voice.

JT looked like he was about to say something as the drill turned his back to walk out, but I shook my head at him to keep quiet. The drills smoked me for only a few minutes. We both knew I wasn't going to talk even though we both knew I had answers. JT was too good of a man to watch me suffer so he told our drills the truth and said I knew nothing. It was a blatant lie about my knowledge of the situation, but neither JT nor the drills believed a person should be punished for not ratting in that particular situation.

Unfortunately for JT, lying to a non-commissioned officer, or NCO, was a punishable offense. He was kicked out of the leadership room and paperwork was being done to strip his Private First Class E-3 rank to be replaced by Private E-2 rank. He was also put on 30 days extra duty, which meant the drills would have extra work for him even after each long day of training. The next 30 days would suck for JT. As he was getting an initial ass chewing from a drill, I was in the leadership room with Ritalin.

"See dude, its all good," Ritalin said in an attempt to rid my face of rage.

I was seeing red and I knew the room was left to just us by our other bunkmate for a reason. It was a moment that happened throughout basic in different forms for a private to be fixed violently by another private. We never had "pillow fights," which were pillow-cases filled with soap bars used to beat a blue falcon in his sleep. That was a more old-school approach. In our platoon, we just arranged for a room or latrine to be emptied except for the privates that needed to fix a problem. It was just Ritalin standing 15 feet away from me in our empty room and a quiet hallway beside us. Rucksacks and duffel bags stood in my way. I had to beat him to a pulp for such cowardice. As soon as he spoke I B-lined it toward him at a high rate of speed, kicking and throwing everything in my path right at him.

"You fucking coward! Pussy-ass piece of shit!" I bellowed.

He was out the door before the first rucksack hit the ground and no, I have no idea what a "pussy-ass piece of shit" is, but that's what naturally came out during my temper tantrum. I'm actually glad I didn't get the chance to cave his face in, because he most likely would have tattled. Ritalin hid from me until he could request to change rooms from a drill. My platoon approved of all my actions and Ritalin was ignored for the remainder of our 16-weeks of training. Even the drills knew what had happened and ignored my attack. In that moment I had to take a relationship with a friend and ask if it was worth the risk of losing rank. I chose my friend. Life in the military would put me in several different situations with these options. JT's situation was the easiest decision in 6 ½ years of service.

Revenge!

"Here's your completion coin, private. Whoopty fuckin' doo da day," DS Gomer said to a private after our last road march in basic. "Oh look, here's another one, woo hoo. This was so hard I know. You gonna write home to momma about this?"

Gomer was a reservist drill sergeant covering for our beloved DS Anderson while he was away for a week. We knew that last march wasn't hard, but we were all proud to complete *something*. Few of us had ever rucked that far with that kind of weight on our backs. Gomer was being very disrespectful and coming from a reservist towards soon-to-be active duty privates, we were enraged. Time to make moves. We could all tell that none of the active duty drills cared too much for Gomer's unearned arrogance. 4Th platoon gathered that night to hatch one last plan before leaving for our units.

"Anyone know when Drill Sergeant Anderson gets back," I asked.

"He definitely said he'd be back in a week and that was a week ago tomorrow," added JT.

"You sure is good at math, JT," Washington joked.

I laughed as JT shook his head at Washington. What a team.

"Then lets nonchalantly slip in what Gomer made of our proud moment as soon as Drill Sergeant Anderson calls his first formation when he gets back," I suggested.

"Yeah 'cause you know he's going to ask us how it went," said JT.

"'Cause he cares," Washington said emotionally.

"And you're making fun of me?" asked JT.

"Yeeeeeah," smiled the big bear of a man, Washington.

Anderson returned the next morning all happy and excited to hang out with his favorite platoon. Although his way of showing love was quite vulgar. Nonetheless we had our *real* drill back. Game on, Gomer Pile, gaaaame on. Anderson called for morning formation and the day went on, but Gomer was always close by so we couldn't talk to Anderson. He couldn't stand Gomer, but he was buy-the-books like SGM Beurns and wouldn't let us speak poorly of Gomer while in his presence. Anderson would just tell us, "Shut up, privates!" We decided to just act docile until Anderson couldn't take it anymore. Finally, after dinner chow, Gomer took off for the night and Anderson called a formation. We had no idea what was going on, because we never had a formation at that late hour.

"Alright, privates. You've been running around all day like somebody pissed in your Cheerios. Riddle me this, *BATMAN*! How can that be? You're about to graduate. Speak your miiiiind, privates... or I'll sweat it out of ya one last time."

Well shit, boss, that's all you had to say! JT's hand shot up and his chest flew forward in excitement to spill the beans on Gomer.

"Well don't blow your load, private. Go ahead," Anderson said.

"Yesterday, we were all proud. I mean, I know it's nothing compared to what we're about to do, but it was something we all accomplished together and Drill Sergeant Gomer was making fun of us during the entire ceremony," JT explained.

"What did he do, though?"

"He made fun of us while handing out our coins and basically saying we ain't shit."

"He's right. You ain't shit... but it doesn't mean he should say that to you. It's a moral killer and I'll fix this, privates. Lights out! Move!"

A few days later, Drill Sergeant Anderson came over to us smiling and frowning at the same time. He was proud of us, but had to remain a hard-ass. I saw Sergeant Major Beurns in the background by the pit. He wasn't saying a word, but had wide-open eyes and a crazy smirk. SGM Beurns was smoking the dog piss out of Gomer in the same fashion he smoked PR. Glory!

"THAT'S WHAT YOU GET WHEN YOU FUCK WITH MY PRIVATES... PRIVATES," ANDERSON STOICALLY, YET AWKWARDLY STATED.

And that's how basic ended.

CRAZYHORSE

After 10 days off following basic, I was headed across the country to my first duty station. I landed at SEATAC airport between Seattle and Tacoma, took a shuttle to Fort Lewis and waited in reception for a month until I was assigned to a unit. I was assigned to Crazyhorse Troop in 1/14, 3rd Stryker Brigade Combat Team in the 2nd Infantry Division. We sported an Indian head patch with a star behind it. I felt excited to meet everyone and train up as soon as possible. What I found was a unit that was the first of its kind that had just gotten home from a deployment in late 2004 and they were in no mood, or mentally stable for that matter, to integrate new guys. Well "gee whiz" lets go get initiated!

Let the Beatings Commence

"Hey Vance, I'm going to smash this clipboard over Opey's head unless you want me to smash it over your head," Staff Sergeant (SSG) Fergie said.

"You can hit me, just don't fuckin' miss my forehead," I stated.

Opey was already hiding in the fetal position in the arms room when Fergie approached me with this proposition. Fergie was a tall, out of shape, backwoods bigot that took advantage of his E-6 rank and the cluelessness of new guys. I had just begun the ritual of initiation.

Fergie raised the clipboard and swung. I simultaneously thrust my head forward as if I was striking a soccer ball. Soccer skills actually came in handy in this situation. If you strike the ball with the top of your forehead, it wouldn't hurt. I took this same philosophy with the clipboard. The clipboard shattered and everyone watching thought I'd be in pain, but I just walked outside of the arms room with a smile.

"You're welcome Opey," I said as I passed thru the doorway.

Opey was an infantryman that had already deployed, so I was a bit curious as to why he was still being picked on in front of a bunch of new guys. He was a tall, thin, redhead that flinched every time Fergie lunged at him. I knew I could start proving myself by making sacrifices and taking beatings to protect other soldiers, but how far could

I take it? I was out of the arms room for a split second when Fergie wanted another round.

"Vance, atten-huh!" grunted SSG Vines.

"We're not done yet, Vance," Fergie said.

There I was, standing at attention in front of 80 guys I wanted to desperately prove my worth to. Vines was staring me down about six inches away from my face to make sure I wouldn't run. When I stared right back as if to say, "bring it" he backed off while smiling with a wad of chew tucked in his lower lip.

"Alright, Vance, alright," he said in a soothing yet scary voice.

Vines was in Raider platoon with Fergie and together they were quite the force to be reckoned with. He was the most diesel looking guy in the troop. He was white, held a Louisiana draw, stood at six feet tall, dipped tobacco constantly and had a gap between his front two teeth. Vines was easily 215 lbs of pure wrecking ball strength. I was fucking screwed.

Vines posted up a few feet away as Fergie walked out of the arms room and grabbed a fire extinguisher. He put the bottom end against my stomach while rotating it with a curious look on his face. I knew exactly why he was sizing it up against my stomach so I flexed my abs and braced for impact. He cocked back and swung with everything he had. *Thud.*

The sound of a hiss came out of my nose as my nostrils flared and I struggled to keep from folding in half. It didn't hurt too badly though. Next. Vines knew I wanted nothing to do with Fergie's approval and could take a beating like that all day, so he picked up a .50 cal barrel. Sucks to be me. Those barrels are 45 inches in length and 24 lbs. Now, if you take a guy that has 65 lbs of muscle on you and he decides to jam you with a .50 cal barrel, you're going to feel it. I stood proudly, but I was secretly screaming like a little girl on the inside. Vines took aim for my navel. Perfect strike.

"Umph," I grunted.

"Hey, hey that's enough now," Sergeant (SGT) Shmiddie said as he walked out of the arms room, "You OK Vancey?"

"Never better," I barely whispered as I gasped for air.

"Go get some air."

Everyone was looking at me with smiles. They hadn't seen anyone take a beating like that without crying about it. A seed was sewn for growing respect from the veterans. Only the new guy beatings weren't done yet.

GOLDEN DROP

I walked passed all of the platoon cages and exited the building. "Fuck, Fuck" games had commenced with the FNG's. Ten guys from my basic training class were assigned to Crazyhorse troop and 35 others were spread throughout the Warhorse squadron. Crazyhorse saw all ten of us as fresh meat. One of the Fuck, Fuck games was assigning a FNG a rock that he had to carry around. If a soldier lost his rock then he would instantly get smoked.

Golden was the first victim in this game. He was thin, freckle faced, brown-haired and possessed the agility of a monkey. Golden had a selective southern draw from being born in Louisiana, but he was raised in Pennsylvania. He only seemed to have a Louisiana accent when somebody said nice things about the south. Golden was a brave guy, but reckless with his actions and his mouth. He was assigned to Raider platoon. What he didn't know at the time was the rock he was assigned would attract the attention of lower ranking veterans who wanted to see him get smoked.

Whitey, a short, strong black guy, took Golden's rock. That's right, a black guy named Whitey. Golden smiled at him and Whitey just walked away with his eyebrows raised as if to say, "You're in trouble now." Golden thought it was a joke since Whitey wasn't a NCO. Golden followed Whitey inside asking for his rock and the rest of us were en tow to watch the outcome as if it were required. Whitey refused to give up the rock and Golden picked it up a notch.

"You better give up that rock," Golden ordered.

Whitey just smiled, forcing Golden to act. What Golden didn't realize is that even though he was in good shape, Whitey had just returned from war. When someone goes off to war and comes back, they have a rage festering inside them. When a combat veteran unleashes that rage, not a whole lot can stop him. Golden towered over Whitey and saw him as an easy target. Golden thought wrong.

Golden came up from behind Whitey and wrapped his arms around him in an attempt to fling Whitey away from the pet rock. In a split second Whitey ducked and got behind Golden. He wrapped his arm around the back of Golden's neck with such a force that Golden bent at the waist and Whitey picked him up in a cradling position, like holding a baby. Whitey then lifted Golden over his 5'8" head and threw him to the concrete floor. I heard the *thud* and turned away.

The *thud* noise was Golden's head making contact with the concrete ground inside the troop, or work area. He was knocked out cold for a couple of seconds with blood starting to form on the back of his dome.

"Shit, now we gotta fix 'em Whitey," Vines said with his thick Louisiana accent.

Raider platoon picked Golden up and took him to the aid station where he told medics, "I fell," like a battered wife as Vines watched him get patched up. He took a beating and protected his superiors. Point to Golden, even though he lost some brain cells that day.

JOHNNY FRANCISCO AND A PINK BELLY

Back at the troop things had calmed down since some officers heard Golden's thunderous fall and came back to the cages to investigate. As soon as the officers left, game on again. I was standing next to the supply cage when I saw John Francisco, or Cisco, examining another FNG. He literally had his arms crossed while circling the FNG and occasionally poking him.

"You're cute," Cisco creepily told the confused new soldier.

I instantly thought he was an asshole. The first impression couldn't have been further from the truth. Cisco was a mortarman of the highest order. He was incredibly smart and took pride in taking initiative. Cisco was one of those guys that had the brains for an Ivy League school, but chose to serve his country instead. He was from Virginia, average height, white, shaved head, smoked and dipped non-stop. For some reason, when he would become inebriated he spoke with a slight English accent, which seemingly highlighted his intelligence.

The first time I saw Cisco I walked into his barracks room to drink with some guys rocking out to Danzig's "Mother." He was sitting in a chair completely passed out with both arms resting on the arms of that chair looking like a worn out Abe Lincoln Memorial except a cigarette was burning away in his right hand. The second time was a different kind of stoic pose. Cisco was in the same chair facing a TV with adult material on and his dick was in his hand instead of a cigarette. Yes, still passed out. As you can imagine, I was curious to see what this guy was like sober.

Cisco didn't see the soldier he was examining as fun enough, so he walked back to the entrance of the mortar platoon office door. It was like a sixth sense that he had. Cisco was a good judge of character and could tell the soldier he was just messing with saw the process of initiation as "not right." Veterans saw initiation as a way to see what we were made of and most of us new guys liked that. It's not the process that counts, but how everyone handles it. We saw initiation as a right of passage and gaining a morsel of respect from people that we looked up to.

My eyes wandered for a few seconds before they met Cisco's eyes. He was already looking at me with that same creepy look he was giving the boring FNG. Cisco flicked his head to the side while chewing a fat wad in the front of his lower jaw. I was thinking "Oh cool, finally someone wants to get to know me." Not exactly.

"Hey there. Come on in and meet everyone," Cisco said as I began my move into the mortars office.

I walked right into the office, which I soon learned was off limits to scouts. Scouts and regular infantry always outnumbered the mortars, so they picked us off one by one. I was just oblivious to that at the time. Being oblivious, as you can imagine, was a common trait among FNG's. I walked into the office and stopped with an awkward smile aimed at everyone that had just stood up aggressively. I saw a metal hanger wire flash in front of my eyes on its way to being wrapped around my neck. Great.

The door slammed behind me and I was instantly grabbed, flipped upside down and slammed against a wall locker while the mortars started beating the shit out of me. It all ended with them flipping my shirt up, twisting my nipples and slapping the hell out of my stomach, a ritual known as a "Pink Belly." Smacking of the belly is no joke. There was blood and chunks of skin missing.

"Welcome to Crazyhorse," they all said with a laugh.

"Well, thanks for that," I said as I limped out of the office half dressed to an applauding group of scouts and infantry.

By day all of the new guys would get their asses kicked and train, but by night the veterans would bring us in to drink with them so as to not ostracize us. We would all gather for a "Barracks Night" on the third and top floor. Some veterans would awe us with war stories, we'd flip quarters off our nasty hallway floor into Dixie cups full of beer and pound them, destroy any exit signs, expend all fire extinguishers, exchange punches to the jaw to see who would get knocked out first, grapple, spar, throw things out of the windows at parked cars and scream at the top of our lungs as blood dripped to the floor. You know, intelligent activities for mature adults. Ok, we were savages... and I loved every second of it.

From the outside this can look like a terrible version of fraternity hazing gone wrong, but I assure you it's a very important step to becoming a soldier and being able to protect the men by your side. The new guys that hid or spoke out against such events were seen as guys not willing to sacrifice a little pride to be a part of a team. If you can't sacrifice a little pride, how the hell are other soldiers going to trust that you'll sacrifice yourself for them in battle? I believe initiation is a necessary evil, so long as there's a stopping point.

BLUE

After a few weeks the beatings fizzled and we could focus more on learning our jobs, except one motherfucker wanted to keep messing with us. Fergie. He really got a rise out of seeing other people suffer. Even Vines would walk away as Fergie kept on with his reign of annoyance. One trick Fergie loved was using an old communications device to electrocute people. It looked like a portable Vietnam era phone attached to a small battery. He would simply touch one end of the phone to someone and then press the "push to talk" button, sending a shock with a snapping sound right at his victim. I was one such victim. Fergie had been threatening me all day and I was tired of it.

"Go ahead, sergeant, but if you do I'll kick your nuts up into your throat," I calmly said with a scowl while standing at parade rest.

"No you fucking won't, Vance."

"Your choice, sergeant."

There was a great silence throughout the troop when this went down as no FNG had talked to Fergie like that. After that exchange, I went down to the motor pool to work on our vehicles. I did my work quickly, visited buddies in other platoons and then started walking down the line to finalize some more chores. This is when Fergie made his move. With my back turned he ran up from behind me.

"Hey Vance," he whispered with his southern draw.

Before I had the chance to turn around, Fergie planted one end of the phone on the back of my neck and pressed to talk. I let out a grunt as I was shocked. Without even thinking I turned around and swung my right leg as hard as I could. As I was turning I didn't care who it was or where I connected with my boot. I ended up connecting with Fergie's crotch and the strike immediately dropped him. I ran for the hills before he had the opportunity to get up. Everyone cheered as I flew by.

Fergie knew I wasn't completely in the wrong for striking a NCO in the balls, so he backed off a little. His next target was Marion. Marion was a beast. He was about 5'10," shaved head, built like a bowling ball of sheer muscle, spoke like everyone else from rural Texas and sported one gold front tooth. Marion was so black we called him "Blue." Blue would always do what was asked of him and Fergie jumped at that opportunity. We always asked Blue to beat Fergie's ass, but Blue would always decline. He was a very chill, quiet soldier.

"Naw, man. Dude's just messin' with me," Blue would protest.

On a slow afternoon, the entire troop was gathered together for more Fuck, Fuck games. Fergie apparently wanted to show off and called out Blue to the center of the concrete floor at the troop.

"Blue! Get in the front leaning rest right there, boa," Fergie salivated.

"Roger, sergeant!"

Blue got into position to do pushups in front of everyone.

"Down!" Fergie yelled as Blue lowered his body in perfect pushup form.

While Blue stayed in the down position awaiting Fergie to tell him "up" Fergie walked up behind Blue on his left side and pulled out a knife. Everyone shook their heads. Fergie then held the knife over the center of Blue's back with the pointy end facing down. "Up!" Blue pushed himself up, not knowing the knife was there, and Fergie gave him a strong stick in the back. Blue cringed as he felt the knife poke him and Fergie just laughed. Voices from the crowd were whispering disapproval.

"Oh I aint really stabbin' 'em," Fergie defended his line crossing actions. "Down!"

"C'mon, sergeant," Blue said as politely as he could.

"Up!"

Blue never came back up. That's where the most obedient soldier drew the line with the most unprofessional NCO. He simply side crawled to the right, stood up and walked away. Good for Blue, but I wanted revenge on his behalf. There would be more instances involving Fergie instigating rebellion amongst the new guys. Slowly we all started fighting back and Fergie eventually learned that nobody respected him. He couldn't punish us under UCMJ (Uniform Code of Military Justice) if he was the one starting shit. During a flag football game between Raider and White platoon, he kept hitting me from behind. I turned around, lunged a shoulder into his beer gut and sent his big ass to the ground. He got the message. Initiations were over. Lets celebrate!

A Knife Fight? Sure, Why Not?

One of my fondest memories while trying to fit in with the veterans as I arrived at my unit was a house party in Seattle. I bought a case of Coors Light and showed up to a bunch of "boo's."

"Coors Light? What the fack is that shit?" Angel joked with his Boston accent.

"I'm guessing this is a Bud Light kinda crowd?" I asked.

"Yeah, leave that shit outside. We got a keg in the kitchen."

I left my silver bullet babies on the deck and ventured in to a world of drunken brotherhood. I got nothing but head nods on the deck and felt awkward. The first thing I saw as I passed thru the doorway was a guy carrying what looked to be a beer bong, but the funnel at the top was unfamiliar.

"How do you like that, Vance," asked Angel.

"What's with the deformed metal funnel?"

"That came off an RPG that got stuck in the side of one of our Strykers. Great souvenir, bro."

"That's so awesome," I oogled.

My eyes were wide open and I was sporting a big smile. I couldn't wait to be able to tell random stories like that. We kept pushing thru the crowded house that attracted the local colleges as well. I wandered into an open area where some new guys were hanging out with vets so I jumped in to hang out.

"Yo, Vance, sit down," said a veteran named G as he stood up to give me his seat.

"Me? No way man, I can't do that. That's your seat!" I pleaded.

"Why aint you takin' that seat?"

"I haven't done anything to earn a seat!"

G laughed, "Yo, we all the same here!"

It wasn't much, but it was the nicest offer I'd gotten in a while. G had E-3 rank, making him lower ranking than me. I came in as an E-4 simply because I had a college degree, which I believe to be the military's greatest tragedy along with certain lieutenants. G was a veteran and I was fresh out of basic training and this man was supposed to be a subordinate to me? Fuck that. I looked up to G and whenever he said something, I listened. G was Hispanic with a thick accent, shaved head, stood about 5'6," lifted a lot of weights enabling him to keep up with anybody and kind of looked like a mini Vin Diesel. He was also the guy I chose to punch me in the jaw during on one of our crazy barracks nights. Poor decision. He even warned me. I swear to this day he was holding back though. If he really wanted to, he could've caved my face in with ease. Across the room I saw some girls pouring beer into a softball cleat. Where there are girls doing silly things with alcohol, there will be curious guys.

"What's with the 'shoe-o-beer'?" I asked

"We're all on a softball team and these new bitches have to drink from it for initiation," one of them proclaimed while two younger girls grimaced.

"Oh damn, that cleat looks used and abused."

"A whole season's worth of use and abuse."

As the cleat was held up for freshman humiliation and people chanting "drink," I ventured into the kitchen. That's where I met up with Yancey Baker. He was sitting on a stool at the kitchen bar with a fifth of Wild Turkey; a substance I hadn't tried before. Yancey was of average height, brown haired, thin, white, proud Alabamian from the mortar platoon who could throw down 'til the sun came up.

"Vance! Come here and have a drink of whiskey with me," he ordered from across the kitchen as I passed the line of people doing keg stands.

"I don't know man," I said.

Yancey then proceeded to take out his left eyeball and hold it on the tip of his left index finger. He then gave me a big grin.

"You mean to tell me you can't sit down and have one fuckin' drink with me at this party?"

"Baker, I'll drink as much as you want me to."

"Aight then."

Yancey then told me the story of how he lost his eye when a car bomb exploded right next to his Stryker as he was standing out of one of the hatches. I got to know Yancey real good that night as I learned of the sacrifices some of us would have to make without having a choice. The fake eye was impressive. Yancey was happy with it, tossed it in his mouth as if to clean it and then put it back in his socket while we both laughed over a bottle of Wild Turkey.

From the conversation with Yancey and my first encounter with Wild Turkey things got a little crazy. After doing a couple rounds of keg stands I was feeling great. All of a sudden I hear one of the vets screaming at a local guy about messing with his girl. Clark was the vet and he was no bigger than I was, but a lot more jumpy. Something about him liking "snow" is what somebody told me, but it was too warm outside for that. I just didn't get it. He did happen to have an attractive girlfriend and with this much alcohol and people, I'm sure someone made a pass at her and Clark wasn't in the right mindset to keep calm about it. Before I knew it, a circle had formed in the kitchen and Clark was threatening a guy twice his size when things took a turn for the worse. The guy pulled out a knife.

I'm not a rocket scientist, but there's not a whole lot your military training can do for you when you're drunk and stuck in a small space with a guy twice your size holding a knife. You're going to get shanked. So what does my dumb ass do? I jump right in front of Clark and start screaming at the guy to make a move. Luckily for both Clark and I, this local was smart enough to realize there were a lot more members of Crazyhorse just waiting to jump in and he only had a few friends. He backed down and left. Clark was impressed I had the balls to try to help and that was enough for me to be happy. It was a wild end to a great night. Even the next day had an extra surprise.

"Where's Rojas?" I asked.

"I'm right here, dude. I just got back," Rojas said as he walked up to the third floor of the barracks.

"Shit man, what happened to you last night?"

"I wandered off, so I guess my ride left me. I woke up on a stranger's recliner a couple houses down from the party."

"Hell yeah."

The day after a crazy night like that we all thought we would chill out and relax. Nope, not anymore. It was taught to us from the beginning that it was a lifestyle to work hard all day and party your ass off all night, every night. It was frowned upon to show up to morning PT without a funny story to tell or reek of booze. As long as we could hold ourselves up, keep our mouths shut and do the exercises, superiors would put up with how the smell of alcohol was seeping from our pores. The weekends weren't even a time to rest the liver. They just allowed more time to booze. Weekend afternoons, especially on three or four day weekends around holidays, brought on a new level of crazy.

Drunk Punch Pow

"Hey Vance, you wanna go muddin' with us?" asked one of the guys in the barracks.

"I dunno man," I replied with curiosity.

"Well do ya, or not?"

"Yes?"

"You never been, have ya?"

"Nope, I'm from the suburbs."

"Wow, grab some clothes you don't mind getting dirty. You're about to have a great time."

Ending that conversation with "You're going to have a great time," would be some famous last words. Cheap tequila was being passed around the bonfire like electrolytes at a marathon. We had been driving all over a wooded area near Roy, WA in the summer of 2005 getting stuck, then unstuck and then stuck again thru heavy mud, swelling streams and rock formations. The weather was sunny and in the high 70's. We had just commenced the celebration of surviving a day with off-road vehicles when out of nowhere, one of the veterans leaped over the bonfire.

"YEEEEAH!" cheered the circle of inebriated people.

"You're crazy," I pointed out.

"And you're next, Vance," another vet called me out.

So, we have a lot of alcohol, a large fire and a guy who can't jump.

These are the ingredients for a poor decision. Lets do this.

"I better have another swig of that tequila first, cause you know my clumsy ass is going to fall right in."

I was sober enough to decide to start my running jump from the top of a hill. Luckily the tequila and Bud Light kicked in as I started my move to numb any misfortunes. Off I went trying to prove myself again. I waited until the last possible second to take the leap. Up in the air I went using my jean-covered legs as a shield for the rest of my body from the heat. Landing safely over the bonfire of pallets wasn't difficult at all. Again? Of course! We leaped and drank well into the night.

"Alright guys, I gotta get back to the house to relieve the babysitter," Able said.

"Boooooo!" we bitched.

"I know, I know."

Able, his girlfriend, Cisco, Rojas and myself crammed into his small SUV. The rest of the group stayed as we made our way down thru the gravel covered country road. Able seemed fine when we left, but how was I to know being intoxicated myself. He was bantering back and forth with his girlfriend, who was in the passenger seat. The two were laughing hysterically and I noticed Able wasn't paying attention to the sharp turn ahead. This sobered me up pretty quick.

"You OK to drive?" I asked.

"Yeah, yeah I got this!" Able answered sounding annoyed.

He then sped up to take the turn. I'm assuming this is a tough guy's attempt to impress his girl.

"Slow the fuck down, Jesus Christ!" Cisco said with authority.

"Shit," Able muttered.

Of course he took the turn too fast and the vehicle started to fishtail. As we violently swerved and Able tried desperately to maintain control, butterflies went ape shit in my stomach and the hairs on the back of my neck went all Teen Wolf on me. Brace for impact. The vehicle finally went perpendicular enough to the road with the right amount of speed and flipped an unknown amount of times. All I remember is the SUV hitting on the side the first time then waking up to Cisco's voice.

"Get off me Rojas. You're fat," Cisco said in his drunken English voice.

The vehicle landed on its side and the three of us in the back were on top of each other with Cisco getting the brunt of the weight. Luckily for me I landed on top of that pile. I crawled out and we helped each other clear the wreckage. I only counted four of us though. Where's Able's girl? I looked around the area and there she was on her knees in the middle of the road about 30 feet behind us. Apparently she flew out of the sunroof when the vehicle went belly up and didn't have a scratch on her.

"Thankya Jaysus. Oh lawd, I thankya!" Able's girlfriend screamed to high heaven in a country accent as we all stammered to check on her.

"Good luck with that tonight, Able," I laughed.

"Oh great," Able replied knowing his girl was going to be an emotional wreck for a while.

Shortly after the car toss, Vines and Phelps pulled up in an old black pickup that Vines had spray painted orange and yellow flames on.

"You guys have fun?" Vines asked.

"Had my ass kicked worse than that," I laughed again.

"You barracks guys hop in."

We collected all the alcohol so Able could leave it overnight without being investigated too thoroughly if anyone found the vehicle before he could get it towed the next day. Vines drove us back to the barracks and I slept wonderfully that night. Mudding was fun, but I need to select a DD with better efficiency.

A couple of weeks later I was propositioned for another trip to go mudding. Of course I jumped at the opportunity to get out of the barracks. This time I went in Whitey's 4-door Durango. Not your typical vehicle to go mudding in, but that thing could take a beating.

After mudding we commenced in the consumption of tasty beverages again. At some point in the night I hit the wood line to relieve myself. Glaze wandered off to do the same thing about 20 feet away and yes, Glaze is his real last name. As I'm marking my territory, I hear the Durango's engine rev up. I turn my head enough to see that Whitey wasn't done mudding yet. He was barreling in the direction that Glaze had walked. It was dark, so Whitey had his lights on and as the Durango started to get some air under it I see Glaze scampering off to the side laughing his ass off. If Glaze didn't move he would have been crushed.

"Glaze, you almost got run over, man!" I yelled thru the woods.

"Heh! Fuckin' Whitey, man," Glaze laughed with a big grin, shaking off the fact he almost got steam rolled.

Brett Glaze was a proud Texan (shocker) of average height, strong, brown hair, blue eyes, no fear and had a crazy streak in him that magnetized other soldiers to his always "loyal to my bros" side. If I were to make my own team of scouts and infantry to go to war with, Glaze would be at the top of my list.

"You good, Glaze?" asked Whitey.

"Yeah, fuck it," he replied still laughing.

It was time to head back. I sat behind Whitey in the back and Glaze was on the opposite side of the back seat with me. Once again, my driver seemed OK. I was wrong... again. As we headed towards Fort Lewis down some country road I noticed we were going too fast for the up coming s-curve. I didn't bother to try and say anything since my attempt the last time this happened went unnoticed. I just braced myself the best I could.

We skidded off the road and hit a tree on Glaze's side of the vehicle. I flew across the back seat and the side of my head slammed into Glaze's broad left shoulder, knocking me out cold. Both windows on Glaze's side shattered and it looked like Chuck Norris did a roundhouse kick between the two doors.

"Vance!" Glaze yelled.

"Yeah? I'm good," I replied in a haze.

"No dude, I've been screaming your name. You were out."

"Shit, well I'm good now," I said with a smile.

"I think I fucked up my shoulder."

I felt the warm sensation of my own blood running down my head and all over my right shoulder. There was a gash on both my ear and my temple. I thought, "This can't be good." That tough Durango wasn't done yet, though. Whitey managed to wiggle the steering wheel while flooring the engine and got the vehicle off the tree we almost wrapped around. We were back on the road. Somehow it rolled back to Fort Lewis. One problem was left. How are we going to get thru the gate with a vehicle that looked like it was at the receiving end of a monster truck rally? It looked like Gravedigger made a violent return. If the gate guards investigated, they would surely smell the alcohol and we would be in deep kimshee.

As we crept up to the gate on a slow roll, Whitey killed the music, but left the lights on to blind the guards while we remained silent and bloodied in the back seat. He came to a stop at a gate guard shack on the left side of the Durango, concealing the damage on the right side. The guard checked our military ID's Whitey gave him, looked at Glaze and I in the back as we hid the blood and smiled like nerds and we were in the clear, or so we thought. As Whitey was taking the ID's back, a second guard came out of nowhere on the right side of the vehicle about 25 feet away.

"Hey. Excuse me! Are you guys OK?" asked the guard.

"We good!" we all said together as the wheels started to turn.

"Fucking go, Whitey!" Glaze whispered.

We all laughed as the two guards shrunk in the rear view mirrors just staring at us in the middle of the road. That second guard saw all the blood and vehicle destruction and then didn't know what to think or do. Luckily for us it was a narrow escape and the Durango was officially retired that night. Whitey dropped us off at the barracks and we continued to drink at the monkey bars while telling Baker about our adventure. We just let the rain wash the blood away.

Doing crazy things on the weekends without any regard for anyone around us was normal behavior. By no means was it right or should it be condoned or popularized, but it's just how people in combat arms tend to handle stress. We were releasing angst we couldn't explain. We just had to do it and not care about consequences for the time being. We would soon be in a war, not knowing if we would come home so why not try living recklessly? Monday was upon us and back to the grind we went. We definitely had a sufficient story to tell during morning PT.

Privates are DUMB

"Hey private," SGT Jindle beckoned.

"Yes, Sergeant!" yelled the motivated FNG.

"Grab me an exhaust sample from that there Stryker."

"How do I do that, Sergeant?"

"You fucking kidding me, private?"

"No sergeant," hanging his head.

"You **START** the vehicle, then you **GRAB** a plastic bag, head to the exhaust and then figure it the **FUCK** out. **ROGER?!**"

"Roger, Sergeant!" and off he went, all motivated to prove himself.

Fuck, Fuck games hath returned. It was performed masterfully. With a straight face a sergeant asked a private to do something that is completely pointless and makes the private look dumb, thus teaching that same private his place on the totem pole. The genius behind the action was acting like the private should have known all along how to get an "exhaust sample." Had SGT Jindle hesitated or smiled, a better private would have picked up on the fact that it was a joke and rendered the act not so funny for onlookers.

"Look at that dummy over there, inhaling exhaust fumes and shit," Jindle gloated.

"He's trying real hard, but let's get him started on another project," SSG Ham suggested.

"Come'ere, you ding-a-ling!"

"Moving sergeant!"

"Well hold the bag tight now, damnit! You're gonna to let the exhaust sample out."

"Where do I take the sample, sergeant?"

"Don't you worry about that. Ya did good so I need ya to make sure there's no soft spots on the armor. Grab a hammer and tap all around the entire Stryker."

"How will I know if there's a soft spot?"

"It'll go **SQUISH**! Now stop wastin' daylight you squirrely little fucker!"

"Yes sergeant!" off he went for round 2 as Jindle discarded the exhaust sample.

Once again, Jindle acted like the private should have known what a soft spot sounded like. The funny thing is, armor doesn't have soft spots. The integrity can be compromised by bullets, RPG's, IED's or rolling the vehicle over, but nothing that goes *"squish."*

Fuck, Fuck games seemed endless as an FNG. Until you had the guts to call out a higher-ranking soldier, you were fresh meat. Another example is making a bad word sound like a legitimate nomenclature for equipment, combining it with a particular higher rank and sending a private off to find it in the direction of a person with that exact rank.

"Hey slap-nuts. Yeah, you," SSG Fergie began.

"Moving sergeant!" Golden replied.

"Go over to sergeant Vines and tell 'em I need a PRC E-6."

"Huh?"

"HUH?! A PRC E-6! You don't know what a 'Prick E-6' is? It's an important part to our comms and as a scout you better learn what the fuck it is! Hooooly shit, private!"

Good ole Golden hadn't caught a grasp of the rank system yet. He was under the impression that a PRC E-6 was a piece of radio equipment. PRC was just a made up nomenclature that was pronounced 'Prick' and E-6 was SSG Vines pay grade. Off Golden went towards the scariest staff sergeant in the unit.

"Sergeant Vines?" Golden murmured.

"Wha?" Vines grunted as he spit some dip into a cup with tobacco-ridden drool falling off his chin, adding to the intimidation factor.

"I need to get a... Prick E-6?"

"Whad yew cawl *me*?"

"Nothing, I just need a Prick E-6," still not getting it as we all started to look in horror.

"Naw who sent yew?"

"Sergeant Fergie, sergeant."

Vines looked towards Fergie and smiled, nodding his head as if to say, "Well played, Fergie, well played indeed."

"Well I guess you found one Golden. Sucks to be you. Just start beatin' your face."

And the pushups began as Golden then realized he just called a NCO a prick right to his face. There you go, just let it sink in. He might not be smart but at least he'll get strong along the way.

When you combine being naïve with a high motivation level, you get all kinds of results. I was caught up in one such event and it was a failure of epic proportions. My platoon was about to train in the field for a few days as the sun was setting at Fort Lewis. Yes, I said the sun, or B.O.B. (bright orange ball) as we referred to it since nine months out of the year brought us cloud-laden skies. It happened to be the first time I got to be in the gunner's hatch. I knew very little about the .50 cal at the time and never even touched the thermal sights that had to be installed on top of the weapon to accurately fire at night, which was coming up on us very quickly. What's even worse is that I didn't know how to mount the equipment that attached the thermal to the weapon. Now why didn't I know how to efficiently operate this equipment? Aw yes, because my first-line supervisor was a turd that never taught me anything.

"Eh Vancey-poo," Shmiddie chirped.

"Sergeant?"

"Yeah, go ahead and put the PAS-13 up."

"I've never seen the mount for it before and don't know how it goes on, sergeant."

"Well it's getting dark so just... figure it out ya food stamp."

I realize a monkey could probably do this task, but if you've never seen the mount, it actually looks backwards when properly attached to the .50 cal. Fuck it. I'm a motivated go-getter that gets shit done and if he's not going to teach me, then I'm going to tear this weapon to pieces in defiance... then play dumb. I took out my military issued Gerber and went nuts. I got the mount on in a way that looked normal. The bad news is that it was at the expense of the rear metal sights which were attached to a plate that was internally attached to a part of the weapon that makes it go, *'pew, pew, pew'* or more accurately, *'thun, thun, thun, thun, thun.'*

"Sergeant Shmiddie, we have a problem."

"How's that? You're my Vancey-poo."

Cheesy terms of endearment... not helping your case for worst leader ever, buddy.

"I had to unscrew the rear sight plate to make the mount fit."

"It aint called a rear sight plate."

"Well then that *thingy* right there."

"You fuckin' smart ass. You're so cute when you're pissed."

I just stared with a face that can only be described as, "When my patience runs out, you're getting punched in the throat."

"Vance, these screws are supposed to be permanently stamped in and a Gerber can't get them out."

"I'm telling ya that's all I did."

"Well I'm not that pissed even though you dead lined the weapon, 'cause I ain't ever seen someone do this. I mean, nevers."

Thanks for the poor English lesson.

"Soooo am I in trouble."

"Nah I'll make somethin' up to tell Pons (our platoon sergeant). Just put up the 240. And shit man, next time just ask for help."

REALLY?! Guess I didn't make it clear enough earlier. At least he covered for me? Even though he created this mess? After that I just taught myself and can do all tasks in my sleep, but if you don't show someone how to use an object they've never seen, the results can be... no bueno.

Among some of the stranger instances with new guys was with Lynus. He was serial-killer quiet, average height and weight, brown hair, Elmer Fudd style face, always had his head down and on the rare occasion he would speak, it would be some weird request like, "Don't stand so close," even if the group was ten feet away with their backs to him. We were uncertain if he was talking to himself, an imaginary friend or us. My friend Dan was stuck as his roommate while in 3rd Platoon.

"I can't take it much longer!" Dan said all fired up, flailing his arms.

"Lynus use your deodorant again?" I asked.

"I wish he would."

"Did he poop his pants in the room?"

"Nah, he..."

"Did he cry for his momma all night?"

"Shut up! The whole fucking room wreaks!"

"Hahaha! Sorry man, it's just funny seeing you rage."

Ever since basic we knew Lynus was a dirty bird. He never got undressed in front of anyone during our 1 minute of shower time. Apparently one night he was scene wiping his body down at a sink while wearing his tighty brown underwear the military issued. All the while strategically wiping inside his underwear so he wouldn't actually be scene naked in front of anyone. Fucking weird. Lynus was that guy you didn't want to piss off though, because you didn't know how he'd react. One day at the motor pool...

"Lynus. You know you're wearing a winter top with summer pants?" asked SSG Ham.

A hush goes over the crowd and Lynus' head goes lower than normal to evaluate his pants situation in the wintertime. He doesn't respond, which is a bad idea for an FNG when a seasoned SSG speaks to you. Lynus' summer pants were faded and you could see the normal white lines resembling the stitching always seen on summer pants. His top was darker and fresh, which is typical for winter uniforms, because we didn't like using them for breathability purposes. This made it very easy for a veteran like Ham to see the mistake Lynus made with his fashion selection.

"It doesn't matter if you wear summer BDU's in the winter or winter BDU's, but man, pick one. You can't mix and match."

Silence.

I'm standing about 30 feet away with 2nd Platoon as I can faintly hear Ham ripping into Lynus in his own quiet way in front of 3rd Platoon. All of a sudden I see Ham lean his head towards Lynus, squinting his eyes as if he's examining something. Then Ham's head cocks way back and his eyes were wide open. He walked towards my platoon shaking his head and eyes still wide.

"What's going on, buddy?" J.D. asked Ham.

"I... I just don't know how to handle that."

"Handle what?"

"Crying."

"By crying..."

"Fucking tears and shit. All I did was point out that he's wearing an inappropriate uniform and he's tearing up over there. I didn't even yell. I mean, what am I supposed to do with that?"

Lynus was so mentally deep in his own world that he couldn't fathom the idea that he could make mistakes. When Ham pointed this mistake out in front of his platoon, it literally ruined Lynus' world. That was the only emotion I would ever see come out of Lynus in the four years I knew him. No laughing, yelling or singing. Just straight faced and monotone, besides that one day Ham was able to breach whatever delusional walls were put in place. You meet all kinds of folks in the military and that was one of the strangest guys I encountered.

These were just a few of the guys I went thru basic with. Most of us were good shit. As time passed and I was able to prove myself in training, I was promoted to sergeant. It was something I was very proud of and the idea of leading men into battle suited me. Now, what kind of men would I be leading? Mouth breathers? Psychos like Lynus? I was in for a rude awakening with my first batch.

My 3 Little All-Stars

Our unit was six months from deploying when I was assigned my first three soldiers that were all mine. Of course, these soldiers were the biggest idiots I'd ever met. I thought I was being punished for something.

"No Vance, we just think you're the only one that can fix them," SFC (Sergeant First Class) Pons, our platoon sergeant, said with a smile.

Every group has a problem child mixed in with good soldiers to dull the pain. All I had were three problem children, a dunce for a first line supervisor and nobody to be proud of or look up to. That's what happens when you're the newest NCO. I kept a positive attitude, but soon realized being positive doesn't fix stupid. Fuck my life for the next six months.

We'll name the three mouth breathers Lemon, Lover and Mango. Lemon was a scout of average height, lackadaisical, clumsy, well fit, light haired and an overall male ditz. He reminded me of a five year old who says he wants to be a fireman one day and the next day he wants to be an astronaut. That's great kid, just let me know when you're all gown up and know what the fuck you're actually going to be. By describing him as "well fit" I mean he had what we called "re-tard strength." You need over a hundred pounds of ammo lifted over your head to load onto the trucks? Lemon!

Mango had the same retard strength, but the demeanor of a Neanderthal. A white, backwoods, gorilla-shaped scout from Minnesota who always had tall tales of crazy hunting days with some character he called "Gunner Nelson." Mango couldn't just say "Gunner" or "Nelson" either. Both names had to be used together. He graduated in a class of seven. Seven... and he wasn't even the runner up for valedictorian. Imagine a guy that thinks he's fooling everyone with lies about how awesome his life in Minnesota was. Now imagine him telling these lies with that hilarious accent from a state with thick Canadian-like tendencies.

"Oh yaw, Gunner Nelson and me would go out fer days hunting!" he'd say all excited as we would all just smile and nod with an awkward silence.

It would only be stories about Gunner Nelson from his hometown. Ole Gunner Nelson sounded more like an imaginary friend, but I guess that's to be expected with a graduating class that was three times smaller than our platoon. I tried, but had a hard time relating to his hunting stories. I was from the suburbs where fishing was the closest thing to hunting as I ever got while growing up. Mango was one of many characters I would have to study to find out what motivated him to function as a soldier in order to allow our little group to work smoothly.

Then there was Lover. Holy shit. *This* guy. Lover was quite the abomination and even in his absence, he would provide us with hilarious stories while deployed. He was a slow moving, short, frumpy Hispanic infantryman from Los Angeles with a thick accent from somewhere south of the boarder. It took a serious effort from him to look like he was awake and not a complete bag of ass. Lover was a terrible soldier and frustrating as hell to work with, but he had the most hysterical stories about his girlfriend. I mean, they weren't funny to him, but I was usually in tears laughing at how crazy she was while listening to his accent.

"Like, this one time, my girl wanted to get freaky in bed so she told me to let her fall asleep and then wanted me to fuck her awake. So I did! She freaked out and screamed at me to stop raping her," Lover said with a sad look on his face that turned to a smile for the ending comment of his story, "but I fucking *lov'er*, man."

Lover would end every story with those words. You can't make this shit up. I couldn't believe the stuff that would come out of his mouth. We all had a hard time understanding why he would put up with this chick. He'd begin every story with words of wonderment.

"Like, this one time, I walked two miles to McDonalds to get her breakfast in bed and she told her cousins to jump me. So they did! But I fucking *lov'er*, man."

"Why the hell did she tell her cousins to do something like that?" I'd enquire.

"I don't know, maybe because I raped her."

"But she told you too!"

"Yeah, but I fucking *lov'er*."

Just imagine a bunch of us listening to this. One guy would slap his own forehead, another would put his head down in disbelief, another would tilt his head like a confused dog and the rest of us would just stare with our jaws down.

"Like, this one time, she said she was going to kill my mom."

"Alright dude, that's a deal breaker."

"But I fucking *lov'er*, man."

"Holy shit. Just stop."

Eventually that crazy little firecracker would use all $20,000 of Lover's enlistment bonus on jewelry shortly before dumping his ass while he was at Fort Lewis and she was in LA. Lover was already a mess, but that didn't help. He took a dull knife to his wrist one night. Lover called another platoon member shortly before he did it, so we don't know if it was a legit attempt or a cry for attention. Either way, that was a one-way ticket out of the platoon as we were too close to deploying for mental issues. His actions left us a man down in an already small platoon. Something that I'm sure didn't go thru his mind as he sawed at his wrist. We missed Lover's stories after we took off for Kuwait and Iraq, but he was certainly the weakest link so we were able to pick up the pace. Or would we?

As soon as we got to Kuwait I found out that Mango had an issue with his enlistment contract. He was supposed to receive a bonus after enlisting for active duty from the National Guard, but never did, thus making it a breach of contract. Mango's options were to either leave the military due to the breach or reenlist for nothing. Both options were crap. Mango had a kid on the way and needed the money, but on the other hand his current job was quite hazardous and making it home wasn't guaranteed.

Being so close to moving into Iraq, most of the platoon would brand Mango a coward if he decided to go home. He was my soldier; therefore I had to give him that older brother advice. I told him he had a family on the way and it was his responsibility to take care of them. Of course the decision was his, but I reiterated the most important thing in life is family. Mango could stay and earn money with benefits. Some of us morbid bastards thought about how the military's $400,000 life insurance would take care of his family too. He decided to go home and I supported him, even though his decision was not what any of us would have done had we been in the same situation.

Where did all my advice and support get Mango? That piece of shit went home, cheated on his girl and then left his own kid in the dust. The last time anyone saw Gunner Nelson's best friend, he was lurking in some bushes outside an apartment complex in Tacoma claiming to be hunting squirrels. My trust in people doing the right thing started to slide downhill and I hadn't even been in a firefight yet.

Out of my three turd nuggets, Lover was being kicked out of the military because he "*fucking lov'er*" and Mango would be sent home shortly to cheat on his woman. This left me with Lemon. To his credit, if I ever asked him to do something, he'd do it real fast like. I could tell him to run into a door full speed and a few seconds later you'd hear the crash. I had just been promoted to sergeant so it was solely on me to keep this guy in line. Oh how I hoped for better soldiers in the future. Would I ever get relief?

Hey Kuwait, Nobody Likes You

Flying into Kuwait, I was in awe of the oil fields that I had only seen on TV. My sense of adventure kept my forehead glued to the plane window.

"Welcome to Kuwait," Drew sarcastically said passing by as he slapped the smallpox vaccine scab on my shoulder.

"What the fuck, man? That was on my smallpox shit," I whined.

Drew turned to look at me, his eyebrows raised and then he turned away quickly. I turned to see what he was looking at. Yep, it was our squadron commander, Lieutenant Colonel Peterson. He was just looking at me so I smiled, awkwardly nodded and turned back around and walked over to Drew.

"Thanks a lot asshole."

"You're the one that said it."

Kuwait was the final training spot for our unit in June/July 2006. We would acclimatize while checking our equipment and make sure we were all on the same page for every situation we could think of. You know what's awesome about Kuwait? Nothing.

Stepping off the plane and onto the tarmac I thought, "This plane's engines need to be turned off." There lies the problem. The engines *were* off. As I walked off the tarmac towards the buses it felt like an angry hairdryer was glued to my face. I had a hard time opening my eyes with the heated wind and of course fucking B.O.B. was there leaning on us at 120 degrees. That's quite extreme considering we left Fort Lewis, WA at about 55 degrees then Maine then Germany en route to "The Sandbox." We had to wait to get on the buses, so we gathered under some tan netting and hydrated. I was in the shape of my life a couple days earlier, but with a slight hangover, jet lag and smallpox vaccine symptoms kicking my ass I had a hard time breathing in that climate. I thought "There is no way I'm going to make it a year in this air *and* fight in a war."

Our days were long, but simple. We would get up around 3am to avoid the extreme heat while working out. Then we'd eat, hydrate and go straight into training until about noon. Then we'd hide in the tents where the temps were at a nice, cool 95 degrees. Guys would clean weapons, do classes on scouting, play cards or sneak off to the port-o-john with porn to rub one out, which was gutsy because you could easily become a heat casualty doing that.

Fighting fatigue from that damn smallpox shot along with an unnecessary anthrax shot, we made it to our home for the next few weeks. It was a tent that would house about 85 sweaty, nasty dudes who would often forget they were about to enter a war zone with each other. Being away from home, no women, no booze and training we didn't need was the perfect equation for short fuses to fly off the chain. On top of all that, we slept six inches apart on cots. Of course there were messy guys that didn't believe in personal hygiene or keeping their 6 x 2 ft area organized. Real hard, I know.

We would rotate a two-man guard around the clock on the Strykers and do maintenance. This was a particularly annoying task considering the trucks were parked about a half-mile away and the path to them was nothing but deep sand. I remember carrying my MK 19 to the trucks one day. It weighed 75 lbs and the only comfortable way to carry it was to front-load it. That equals a great arm workout since the walk took 15 minutes thru the deep sand.

While pulling guard on the trucks at night we would stare off into the black abyss of night and wonder what was happening across the boarder to the north. We went to the range just one day. The range consisted of us driving 30 minutes to the middle of nowhere, passing a herd of camels and shooting at paper targets set up in front of some sand burms. Life in Kuwait got boring real quick. To top it off we were introduced to a Middle East tradition, the sandstorm.

One day while bored out of our minds at the trucks, we tested the theory that if you wet a sock, put a bottle of water in it and then lay it in a shaded area that the bottle of water would significantly cool down. It might have just been a trick on the mind, but it seemed to work. Simple things like this made us look like a caveman grunting at the discovery of fire, "*ugh, ugh!*" While we were laughing at our own simpleton ways I looked off into the distance as the wind kicked up.

"The hell is that?" I asked.

We all stood slowly and looked to the horizon. It was some kind of haze moving in our direction. Haze my ass. It was a seven day sand storm. Sandstorms are the most annoying things on the face of the planet. Even more annoying than Jim Carey's "most annoying noise in the world" routine in "Dumb and Dumber." You can't hide from it. It has sustained winds like in a hurricane, but much weaker of course. Winds would consistently stay in the 20-30 mph range. Sand coated everything and cleaning weapons became difficult. When it finally settled, we rejoiced.

The days continued and seemed to get longer and longer. People in leadership positions, such as SSG Breastos, tried to come up with ways to keep the rest of us busy. Instead of succeeding, he only infuri- ated us with "hip pocket training." It was a term used to tell a guy in my position to pull a class out of his ass to teach the rest of the guys. We all knew the material, but we had to look busy in the presence of rank that was above Breastos so it didn't look like his soldiers were getting lazy. We'd also just get sent to the trucks to "disappear" for a little while.

At night the temperature in the tent would actually drop to what the AC was set at, a frigid 65 degrees. Some guys would bring their cots outside to sleep. It doesn't seem bad, but when you're used to 120 degrees outside and 95 degrees inside, that 30-50 degree drop will shock the body quite a bit. It got agitating as the time grew near to push north.

We were initially told we were going to Anbar Province in western Iraq, a desolate region. Our "torch party," or soldiers that went early to start our transition with the unit currently in that area of operation had already arrived at that destination. It didn't take long before rumors started to fly about our unit not going to Anbar anymore. I would always find a reason to get into our higher command's tent to listen to radios and look at maps to get an idea of where we might be going. I don't think anyone had a fucking clue.

We were about to move north and be a part of the surge of American troops in Iraq at the height of the war. The rumors floating around were Baghdad. Fuck yeah! To the center of the shit. We were told not to talk about it so of course some "Joe" was at the phone booth telling his girlfriend how important he was and where he was going. That led to him walking out of the phone trailer and immediately being escorted off. Not his best move. Excitement was at a peak!

Wanting to keep as much packed as we could to be ready to move at a moments notice, we froze our asses off in the tent. Thankfully it was on the first night of sleeping without fart sacks (sleeping bags) or puss pads (sleeping pads) that we got the word. Off we went to get on the C130 plane for Baghdad. For once the rumors were spot on. My adrenaline started to move thru my body like the constant flowing lava on Hawaii's Kilauea volcano. Here we go. Fuck you, Kuwait. Hello, war.

15 STRAIGHT

I didn't care how long I was going to be gone. All I wanted to do was experience war by saving innocent lives and killing bad guys. Death wasn't a fear, but cowardice was. I had never been shot at so I had no idea how I would react under fire. It was a restless time and I can't think of anything more exciting. We were all ready to find our spot in the world and this was our generation's war. All the training and nights sleeping in the cold rain were over. This is our time... our moment in history.

Welcome Mat

"Put that away," ordered the C-130 crewman as I exited the plane on a Baghdad runway.

"Oh, it's not even turned on," I lied about the camera being used to document my war adventures that was strapped to my vest.

"Alright."

Sucker.

To make sure OPSEC (Operational Security) was maintained, we weren't allowed to take pictures or record anything like air bases. Thanks a lot social media. We walked off the long runway and set our gear down at a smaller tarmac to await the "shithooks," or Chinook helicopters to take us to FOB Falcon off route Irish, or Jackson. It was 115 degrees in the sun, which was nice compared to the 125 average in Kuwait. Still sweaty with some stank though. As we sat on top of our gear baking in the sun, a VBIED (Vehicle Born IED), or car bomb, blew up at one of the entrances to the airport.

"Congratulations, ya'll just earned a combat action badge," Bendel muttered.

We all laughed, knowing the award had lost its bravado and some POG's literally would have tried to claim one on that explosion a few miles away. Bendel received his probably around the same time he got his purple heart for taking multiple RPG shrapnel wounds to the face and continuing to stay in a fight until his own blood blinded him during his first deployment in 2003-2004. Sirens went off as ambulances raced to the scene of the car bomb.

"Oh look, there goes the secondary bombs," joked another NCO.

We laughed again, only this time after a short chuckle I realized I wasn't yet numb to the danger around me like the veterans were. I still wondered how to tactically avoid a fucking car bomb, much less a secondary or even a tertiary bomb. A silence blanketed us once again as this realization sank in for everyone.

The shithooks came in as night fell and we all ran up the ramp as the heat coming off the bird singed our faces and we piled on top of each other. I was the last man on and sat next to the ramp with the gunner who was sporting a 240B machine gun. All the lights on the bird were out as the pilots used NODS (night vision goggles) to see and up we went over Baghdad. I was in awe and enjoying the view. Then shit got real.

The ramp never went all the way up so the gunner could shoot to protect the bird. Imagine a 15ft x 10ft open space with wind swirling all around and that's what was only a few feet away from me as I noticed the gunner holding his headset and screaming into his mic to communicate with the pilots about something. All of a sudden I saw tracer rounds coming from the city only a few hundred feet below and the shithook released flares, which were quite a surprise to the fresh faced guy sitting next to the gunner. I wasn't sure if they were counter measures or if the gunner needed to see below, but they made me jump real high in the seat.

The gunner took aim at something, but never fired as the bird went ass down and I was staring very vertically at the city. I guess it was a defensive maneuver by the pilots. I used a kung fu ninja grip on the cargo netting to keep from falling and kept eyes on the gunner incase he fell out of the bird as I was going to take the gun next. Thankfully he was attached to a safety cord at his waist to hold him in. The shithook leveled out after gaining some altitude then took us for a nosedive just minutes later.

"Really wish I knew what the fuck was going on outside this deathtrap!" I yelled to the man next to me, who of course couldn't hear a damn thing. He just smiled and gave a thumbs up. Nope, he didn't hear me.

The nosedive took us right into Falcon. We were told to run off the birds and get to cover. So what did we do? We ran right past concrete bunkers and into tents. Tents. I say again, tents. You know what those tents had for protection? Cots. We bunked up with some of our guys from White platoon that arrived a little earlier to get the Strykers ready for combat.

"Well, how was your day, sweet cheeks?" I asked Golden.

"We were working on the trucks and started taking small arms fire from I don't know where," he replied.

"Everyone OK?"

"Yeah, we just dove behind some tires 'til it ended and went back to work."

I didn't even have a map of the AO and we were already getting attacked in the Doura area of southern Baghdad. I found a cot, shoved my gear underneath and shut my eyes. About ten minutes later I heard a strange whistling noise. I opened my eyes in the dark tent and frowned at the ceiling. Then an explosion close by. I sat up and looked around as more whistles came. A mortar attack, or indirect fire, had commenced from the city across the street. Boom, *Boom,* **BOOM, BOOM** as dirt and debris rained over the tent. I looked around the tent as all eyes were open, but nobody was doing anything.

"Should we be moving to a bunker?" I asked.

"Hahahaha!" went the veterans.

"What?"

"Welcome to Iraq," SFC Pons confidently replied.

The next night we were scheduled to roll out into sector with the unit that had been there for the past year. They had a different demeanor than we did and I only assumed it was because they had been in combat so long. Soon I would find out it was quite the opposite.

"Vance, you'll be on the ground with me once we get into the city," Shmiddie said.

"Roger," I returned with a smile. Scouts love moving on foot.

We loaded up into the Strykers and followed the little hmmwv's into Abu Disheer. I was on the inside of the Stryker peeking thru one of the hatches above. Dust clouds poured in as I caught glimpses of the tops of buildings and palm trees lit up by a few remaining streetlights. I felt the vehicle stop.

"Driver, drop the ramp. Vance! You're up! Possible IR laser in front of us to detonate an IED! Dismount and check it out!" Shmiddie yelled from above.

"Roger!" I yelled all fired up for action.

Wait... IR? As in infrared? The streetlights blurred out my NODs so all I could use was the naked eye and the naked eye can't see infrared. Can we talk about this? Fuck it. By the time I finished that thought process I was jumping off the ramp after surfing it to "save the day." I was an idiot.

"Vance, don't go too far away from me," Shmiddie whimpered.

"Sergeant, if you step on something that goes 'boom' I don't want to be anywhere near you," I recommended.

"That's fucked up."

"You want to be near me when I trip this IR shit?"

"Good point."

Now as we're checking out the road ahead I notice my view from the inside of the Stryker with "palm trees" was skewed. Trash. That's all I saw and smelled when I jumped off the truck. Some piles were on fire and the smell was awful. Animal carcasses and human body parts were mixed in and it stained everything we wore. It probably wasn't too healthy to inhale either. That being said, I couldn't wait to light up a Newport. There were no lights on in any of the buildings and guess what surrounded those buildings... more trash.

Veterans back at Fort Lewis told us that anything could be used as an IED, so don't go around touching things that you didn't need to. Well, what else do I see when we're walking down the street? A veteran, JD, walk over and kick the living shit out of a styrofoam box the size of a 32 inch tube TV. A space an IED could easily fit into and was actually used often. It was no love tap either. JD's foot, attached to his 6'5" frame, went above his head as he followed thru as perfectly as a field goal kicker. I started moving away from JD with a good pace.

We cleared the street and loaded back up. As we're riding along I eaves drop on the conversation between Shmiddie and his counterpart from the other unit as they stood out of the hatches. Shmiddie got info on all the routes and then asks about enemy contact.

"Our first week here we lost two chaplains and seven men so we made a deal with J.A.M. (Jaysh al-Mahdi Militia) to leave us alone as long as we left them alone," the NCO said.

Shmiddie just looked at him and replied, "Oh." An American unit made a deal with the very people that were killing us. Cowards. We would turn that part of Baghdad upside down for the next 9-10 months, but damn we were off to a rough start in the first 48 hours. We were in a world that made no sense and that fact was the only thing that made sense. I just thought back to the tent that was to be our "cover" for the first week when there was a comment that summed everything up, which would go on to keep me sane in a very sick and demented way.

"Welcome to Iraq."

Crazy Ivan

Between missions, or while on QRF (Quick Reaction Force), I always got a kick out of hearing stories from my guys about their hometowns. Even Mango's imaginary friend Gunner Nelson and Lover's girlfriend stories made me laugh a few times in those turds' absence. Then again, maybe it was just their thick accents talking about it. If you're going to make it a long period of time with the same group of people in small quarters, you better understand where they came from or you might end up killing each other.

Espinal, or Easy E as we called him, was from Queens and when he told me about growing up in his neighborhood I always convulsed with laughter. If we ever had a bad day, we would ask him to tell us about "Crazy Ivan." His story goes like this... oh and keep in mind he has a New York City accent while telling this tale... so again, it goes like this...

"Ok, growing up in Queens was a good time with all my crazy Irish friends that corrupted me and taught me how to play street hockey. Everyday after school we would play street hockey or tag football. After the games we would hang out on my friend Pat Parsley's front stoop and chill, get drinks, et cetera. Well everyday of the week this crazy old junky named Ivan would pass by and harass us and tell us to, 'Get the fuck out of the way,' or, 'Move your fuckin' hockey equipment you shmucks!'

"Wait. Shmucks? People actually use that word?" I interrupted.

"Hell yeah, man. I mean, we called him 'Crazy Ivan' for a reason."

"Touché."

"So we got fed up with this crazy old bum. We noticed that on some days he would walk home with his mom and we could hear her complain about him not having a job. We used this against him on days he would pass by talking shit and complaining to us.

'Hey Ivan, go get a fuckin' job you bum! Quit spending your mom's money on crack! Crack is wack!' we'd yell and mind you this guy was in his 40's.

'Fuck you, you little shits! I have a job! It's to fuck your mothas you little spic, mick bastards! ALL OF YA! I have a job! I don't smoke crack! I smoke your moms pussy!' Crazy Ivan would reply, spilling the beer out of his 40 oz bottle wrapped in a brown paper bag. Ahhh, the good ole days."

"Hahahawwww 'crack is wack?' Really dude?" I'd ask. "Spic, mic bastards? That's not even offensive coming from a crack head! Ohhhh shit… pass the hookah please."

E's hometown story never got old. There's just something about teasing a crazy bum with a potty mouth that makes my day and it sure cheered the entire platoon up. From time to time, all E would have to do is yell, "I fawked ya mothas ya shmucks!" and an eruption of laughter followed.

Drink Piss, then Kiss

Soldiers thought consuming grunt delicacies like JT's hairy caterpillar during basic was another right of passage to becoming a man. I would find great enjoyment knowing this was a ridiculous theory, but in no way would it stop me from instigating further dereliction from normal food entering the intestinal track of other soldiers.

Lets talk about one such soldier named McClurg. He was in third platoon of Echo Troop back in basic. Our platoons shared a hallway in the barracks and did a lot of training together. Although we didn't formally meet until our first duty station at Fort Lewis, I was able to observe his unique character from a distance throughout basic. McClurg was the type of guy that you didn't want messing with you, but it was a riot to see him mess with other people.

McClurg was tall, hefty, skinny armed much like myself, white, dark haired and what he didn't posses in physical attributes he made up for in being quick witted. He also had a larger than average head with abnormal growths, because he was dealing with Gorlin syndrome. Gorlin syndrome causes tumors to grow on the body that can be either cancerous or benign. Either way, these tumors are painful. McClurg dealt with it the best he could and often joked about his big head to make people laugh. On the rare occasion McClurg got under my skin I would just tuck my hands up by my armpits and stagger clumsily like a Tyrannosaurus Rex as if to suggest my head was tough to balance. Yes, if you want to maintain respect amongst your peers while serving in combat arms you have to be twice as brutal as the soldier that crosses your path.

McClurg was a constant source of entertainment in basic. If he wasn't poking fun at somebody, he was questioning whether or not the drills were allowed to smoke us and if certain exercises were crossing any lines. One such exercise in question is known as the "monkey fucker," which is when a soldier bends over, reaches between his legs and wraps his hands around each Achilles tendon. While holding on to his Achilles that soldier would repeatedly squat up and down to make his quads burn. To add a little more humiliation the higher-ranking soldier would tell another soldier to stand behind the guy doing monkey fuckers. The soldier in the rear would then be told to do the "hip rotation!" That entails the rear soldier to put his hands on his own hips, feet shoulder length apart for good balance and then make a circular motion with his hips like doing a hoola-hoop. Yep, that's two soldiers doing soft-core porn in front of a lot of people. Sexy.

With humiliation and pain like that well known to all of us if we misbehaved, I believed McClurg to be very ballsy for breaking out regulation and telling the drills if something seemed out of line. Even though they ignored him, this kind of "questioning the authority figures" infuriated the drills, so they took shots at him whenever they could. One shot was during a class on how to properly apply camouflage face paint.

"McClurg! Eh private, you gonna just use the bright green paint," said a drill.

"Yes, drill sergeant," McClurg said quietly while staring down the drill.

In the summer of 2004 while we were in basic, the Shrek movies were still very popular. Can you already see where this is going? With nothing but bright green paint on his face, an abnormally shaped noggin and a snaggle-tooth on his under bite, McClurg was dubbed "Shrek." Even he laughed. McClurg was a good sport about it and turned it into a part of him. A new character if you will.

With his new persona, Shrek trekked to Fort Lewis, got assigned to White platoon and went off to war. At F.O.B. Falcon in southern Baghdad a mortar attack came in while we had some down time in our old Iraqi barracks and the dirty little bastards hit the jackpot. One of the rounds landed in our ammo point, exploded and set off a large portion of our ammunition. Falcon went into self-destruct mode all over the news and we had to hunker down to hide from our own ammo. You can actually YouTube this. Throughout the night, for several hours, munitions flew at us and exploded. Some of the bigger rounds flew thru other barrack's walls as soldiers ran for dear life. What did my platoon do? We gathered in the hallway to make bets.

With our helmets on and the chinstraps not connected we cheered at every explosion like kids at a Fourth of July show. Never mind that at any second a large artillery round could smash thru the wall, detonate and send us off to the after life. What else could we do? We weren't going to sit around crying about it. I walked into the hall and some of the guys were already trying to collect money for Shrek to drink his own piss. Since the latrines were a far walk, we pissed in empty water bottles called "piss bottles." Creative, I know. Shrek was holding one of his piss bottles filled to about a third of the way. We negotiated to give up a shameful amount of money for him to down it all. With explosions all around and life possibly ending soon, Shrek saved our minds from fear.

"No, no, no! Oh shit, ew, ew, ewwww!" we all gasped.

Seem familiar? Down it went. Only Shrek would take it up a notch. He only took one break then killed the rest of it and grimaced for a moment. Shrek even held it down after a disturbing belch next to a trashcan. We all reacted like we were the stars of a Harlem Shake video humping the air and doing the Pee-Wee Herman dance. Shrek then lifted his head up, stood high, smiled, looked to his right and laid a big ole fat, piss infested kiss on the left cheek of one of our Iraqi terps (interpreters), A.K. Then we commenced with Harlem Shake overdrive.

"Ohhhhhh!" we all yelled as we jumped like crazy.

A.K. was disgusted and I felt kind of bad at first, but A.K. would later betray us by sending phone messages to a town we had to invade. The militia in that town set up several IED's and fighting positions in reaction to A.K.'s messages and a lot of us almost got killed. A.K. wasn't even executed for his treasonous act. He was simply fired and let go. Man, now I wish Shrek had gone even further and licked A.K.'s face with his piss-drenched tongue. Mr. McClurg was king for a day as he helped us get our minds off the thousands of explosions that night. Hats off to him.

Casa de Muerte

"Is that a stick or somethin'?" Shmiddie asked.

"Negative sergeant. That is an arm and hand," I replied.

"An arm?"

"Yeah, a human arm."

"Oh shit."

It was the late Fall of 2006 in southern Baghdad and White Platoon had been getting shot at and tested for a few months. We had a mid-morning patrol scheduled under cloudy skies. As we headed for the gate to go outside the wire, or outside the FOB, nine 107mm rockets hit the base with several detonating close to our Strykers. We pushed thru the barrage and hoped for a new mission plan. We got just that.

The TOC (Tactical Operations Command) informed us over the net that cameras on the blimp had captured smoke plumes where they suspected the launch site of the rockets was and provided us with a grid. We were instructed to move in and investigate. Just 30 seconds later plans changed... again. The camera operators saw two men leaving the possible launch site on scooters and our guys at the TOC would relay their movement to us as this mission turned into a game of "hide and go seek." Oh hello, adrenaline.

We got word that the scooters stopped in a nearby street and the men ran inside a home. I was very pleased to be a dismount on this mission. Our three Strykers surrounded the shack of a home as ramps dropped and we ran out to raid the house. Inside we found two men and two women. The women were acting docile and the men were jittery, but not acting surprised we were there. We took the men outside so we could talk to the women first.

"They say they are very scared of what their husbands will do," said our terp.

"Are those men outside your husbands?" I asked.

"They say no, that is why they are scared of what their husbands will do."

"Did those men say or do anything to you before we got here?"

"They say they were told not to talk to anybody or they would be killed, but they are more scared of their husbands knowing other men were in the house while they were away."

"That's all we needed to know, thank you."

Well I guess that's the one good exception to third world countries not having women's rights. Those women were more scared of their husbands than they were of the men trying to kill fully armed Americans for cash from Al-Qaeda or J.A.M., militants loyal to Muqtada al-Sadr. After a quick search of the shack while questioning the women, we moved outside for the men.

"Separate them and make sure they can't communicate," Shmiddie ordered.

While interrogations of the men commenced, a team of us searched the perimeter for any kind of evidence.

"Eh Sergeant Vance, got somethin,'" Hall said.

"Whatchya got?" I asked.

"Got a video recorder. Might be theirs if we can figure out how to open the video files. Found it over there under that water container."

"A video camera that nice, hidden outside this shack and under a water container? Try to get that thing working, cause I'm betting it has footage of them attacking us."

"Roger."

Hall took Mango's place in our platoon and I could not have been happier. He was everything a NCO wanted in a soldier. Hall knew when to take initiative. That's rare in a new soldier since I usually had to play "Red Light, Green Light" with my previous 3 soldiers when it came to controlling an area. Hall was white, quiet, light haired, average build and from Tennessee with a thick southern accent. He dove right under the water container that all of us had walked past and he hit the jackpot.

"These guys answering questions?" I asked.

"They aren't saying much."

"Got it!" Yelled Hall.

I ran up to Hall and JD as they were examining the footage.

"Motherfuckers," I said, starting to look like Clint Eastwood's face of disapproval.

The footage showed these guys launching all nine rockets at FOB Falcon off route Jackson/Irish. Yahtzee!

"Look familiar?" I asked one of the detainees as I showed him the attempt on our lives.

Both of the men put their heads down and had two completely different stories on why they were in that shack. We blind folded them and put them in separate Strykers while we finished searching the area for more evidence against them.

"Vance, we might have another problem," Shmiddie proclaimed.

"What's up boss?"

"See those wires on the ground? They're a makeshift detonator to a command-detonated device. I'm going to follow the wire to see where it goes. Make sure nobody fucks with that. I don't wanna to get blown the fuck up."

"Got it."

What that means is that Shmiddie saw a red and blue wire

attached to a small, white plastic cap. If these two wires were pressed together, they would complete a circuit. This circuit extended thru very thin, intertwined white and black wires that went into a field. Shmiddie had to find out exactly what was intended on being detonated. I hovered over the wires while he went solo to make sure casualties would be at a minimum in case something went wrong.

"White 4, this is White 3. We got a five gallon drum EFP IED crusted in dirt by a trash pile and need to make this route black ASAP," Shmiddie said on the net.

"3, this is 4. Roger," replied SFC Pons.

To put things into perspective, a coke can sized EFP (Explosively Formed Penetrator) IED can take out a hmmwv. A five-gallon drum would cut a 20-ton Stryker in half. It was resting in some trash on the side of a heavily traveled route. To make that route "black" meant to shut it down.

"EOD is en route," Pons said after reporting to the TOC.

As we waited for EOD, we got another call from the TOC asking that we go to the original grid of the launch site and investigate after EOD showed up to relieve us at the EFP site. We complied. Keep in mind we still have two detainees.

"Sergeant Vance, this asshole won't shut up," Hall said from inside the Stryker.

"He's probably bitching about how we ruined his big payday. First he fires rockets on video and then he tried to obliterate a Stryker. Take a shotgun and charge it one time next to his head. That'll shut him the fuck up," I said back.

Chk, chk! That blind folded detainee sat up straight and about pissed his pants. He thought he was going to be executed.

"That's enough, I don't need them shittin' all over my Stryker," Shmiddie pleaded.

"Mount up White, time to roll," our platoon leader, Captain Kuykendall said.

We found the launch site. There were nine stands from where the rockets were launched and a tenth rocket that never fired on top of a tenth stand. The evidence on these guys was definitely earning them a trip to a dark, small cage. Next to the launch site was a half constructed yellow brick and cinder block house. We dismounted the Strykers and searched the area for more evidence. I started with the unroofed structure.

"Shmiddie what's all this white shit on the ground?" I asked.

"No idea."

I turned a corner and saw a bright blue rope sticking out of the ground. The dirt around it looked fresh. Protocol and common sense was to get a metal detector around suspicious looking things like that in case it was an IED or land mine, but I had a gut feeling it wasn't an explosive. It was way too obvious considering the lengths the two detainees went to conceal their EFP boom boom. Nobody else was in the room so I took a chance with my own life.

I gave the rope a little tug from a distance and it seemed to give way fairly easily, so I got closer and pulled much harder. The rope gave way, I dropped it from my hands and fell right on my ass. I couldn't believe I was staring at a half decayed human arm and hand. After others from my platoon started to come into the room I looked around. It wasn't sticks or kindling to make a fire that was lying around. It was human bones. I had just accidently uncovered a mass grave. The "white shit" on the ground was lime; meant to mask the smell of all the corpses.

"You ok, Vance?" asked Shmiddie.

"Yeah, I just. I don't know. I guess I have a case of the heebee jee-bees, man. I'm gonna smoke by the trucks. Just give me a few."

"Yeah, go for it."

We had come across a lot of dead bodies before and I had no problems, but the idea that so many people were just dumped in a hole got to me. They were a few hundred feet from an entire town and these asshole detainees probably put them there. What the fuck is wrong with these people.

Days like that opened my eyes to how insignificant we all can be in the eyes of monstrous people. In many places around the world, Darwinism takes a dark turn in the name of survival. This is why combat vets are always ready for something to go down and prepared to kill to survive. Its not easy to hide, but just take one look at us when we've been startled by something. All these anti-military activists should go hang out where I've been and I bet they wouldn't be protesting our violent ways ever again. They might even lobby for us to get a raise.

Specialists came in to investigate the scene as we headed off to Cropper, a jail we brought detainees to in the green zone for further "questioning" and "trial." I never got a body count, because there wasn't enough time for the investigators to count them all before dark. It was a busy and productive day for White Platoon. We rolled out with our heads high and happy we were all alive even as the nightmarish scene faded in the distance and the sun set under clearing skies.

"Are we going to eat dinner chow in the green zone before coming back to Falcon, Sergeant Vance?" asked Lemon from the driver's hole.

"Hell yeah, man. I think its Mexican night too," I replied.

"Woo hoo!"

Vagina Mono-WOAH!

There's a famous play called the "Vagina Monologues" in which female actresses play the vaginas of different races and religious backgrounds. One chapter describes what a particular woman says during an orgasm. If I were to add an Iraqi woman to the mix, it would go something like this...

"When a white woman climaxes, she screams 'Ohhhh GOD!' When a black woman climaxes, she screams 'Ohhhh SHIT!' And when an Iraqi woman climaxes, she screams 'Ohhhh... *thump, thump, thump.*'"

"3-Golf, we're moving out, time now," Shmiddie said over the net.

"Roger, the ramp is coming down," I replied.

The sounds of heavy breathing shower over my headset as Shmiddie and his dismounts load up onto the Stryker.

"Looks like you guys had a party," I was suggesting our late night raid had some excitement.

"I... *hugh*... I can't... *hooo*... believe that just happened," Shmiddie gasped.

"Story time!" yelled the driver.

"Shush Lemon," I ordered. "But seriously... story time!" everyone laughs as we haul ass out of the dangerous neighborhood in southern Baghdad.

For months we had been containing the sectarian violence in the muhallas, or neighborhoods, of Abu Dischir and Mechanix in southern Doura across route Irish/Jackson. To put it simply, it was a violent area really close to FOB Falcon. We had a lot of success and a lot of action there. The main four-way intersection was directly between the northern and southern portions of our AO. On the northeast corner, or top right for you directionally challenged people, of the intersection was a "tire shop" that we suspected was home to an individual that kept the enemy up to date on our movements.

We pulled surveillance on the place late at night and noticed he would always be suspiciously looking out of his window during the wee hours of the morning. We couldn't tell if he was looking to link up with someone or if he was scared someone was coming or if the big green tanks on wheels surrounding his home were freaking him out.

One night White platoon decided to "go say hi." The tire shop was on the first floor and the mystery man lived on the second floor. We knew he had a family so we brought along the only American female terp we could find to search any women we might come across. Now this chick was brutal, which was awesome to watch. She was of middle-eastern decent, spoke fluent Iraqi Arabic and knew the culture a lot better than we did.

We had worked with this female terp in the past and watching her question Iraqi women was a show. She would sit them down as we secured the rest of the place and I would hear her screaming in Arabic at the detainee. If she didn't like what she heard… *slap!* Then the detainee would start answering questions.

White platoon roles up and surrounds the place in the middle of the night with no lights and going with night vision, like a good raid should. I was gunning one of the Strykers that night so as I directed my driver, Lemon, to back up towards the building and drop ramp, I see the Stryker next to me drop ramp and the female soldier ate shit bigger than anything coming off the ramp. I had to chuckle because people take for granted how difficult it is to go running off of a moving vehicle using NODS. Plus the NODS we were using, PVS 7's for you high-speed readers, didn't have good depth perception and that drop off the ramp can seem like a mile.

White platoon quietly entered the building and moved upstairs. I could hear screaming from the second floor. Eventually it calmed down. Maybe I heard a *slap* and maybe I didn't, but the screaming stopped. After about 15 minutes, Shmiddie stumbles onto the truck gasping for air with wide eyes. I could tell story time was going to be worthwhile on this night.

"So, as usual, when we go in and start segregating the men from the women and children, the wifey goes nuts on us," Shmiddie starts.

"Butt-stroke to the dome?" I asked.

"Naw, that female soldier shut 'er ass up. Everythang was goin' fine 'til we started findin' ammo and guns and goin' thru them cell phones." (Yes, Shmiddie was a country bumpkin)

"So the mystery man probably freaked?"

"Naw man, it was just the wifey. She exchanged some weird looks with the mystery dude an then it happened."

"Sheeeee went into labor for eleventeenth time?"

"Naw, she fuckin' stood up and 3 grenades fell from her ninja nun dress."

"As in she had interior pockets somewhere?"

"Naw man, I'm telling you they came from between her fuckin' legs. I dunno how, but 3 of them motha'fuckers hit the floor between her feet and luckily the safety pins held up and nothing bad happened."

"Soooo she held them with her thighs?"

"That's the kicker, she was already movin' around before ole girl slapped her in the face. I... I think they were '*up in there*' if you know what I mean."

"Get. The fuck. Outta here," shaking my head.

"That's what I honestly think she did. I mean we're tearing that place apart and if things get desperate... they get desperate. She had to hide them somewheres to help her man, I suppose."

"Were the grenades wet, Sergeant Shmiddie?" asked our demented Lemon.

"Lemon, lets not go there," I pleaded.

After Lemon's question, it was a very quiet ride back to Falcon. We fueled up, parked, dropped ramp and had a cigarette. Nobody said a word. Just a lot of deep thinking with an occasional smirk or chuckle or puzzled looks of men trying to figure out how she did it. Even when someone looked like they had it figured out, they stopped themselves with a caveman grunt and back to a look of confusion.

"Man, I don't... yeah... I got nothin'," I said as we all walked away.

Trash Digger

"You're not gonna like this SGT Vance," a soldier said.

"Whatya got?" I asked

"Bugs have taken to the food."

"Oh, so after 18 hours of a mission gone wrong we have no food?"

"Roger."

"And where is our shit-bird supply guy that was supposed to keep it covered?"

"Sleepin' or jerkin' off."

"Both good excuses to fuck over a platoon that hasn't seen food in a day, right?"

"What do we do?"

"Take the parts that haven't spoiled or bugs haven't taken to and dig into room supplies."

"What are you gonna eat?"

"Just do what the fuck I told you and get some shuteye. We're rollin' back out in a few hours."

I might have been acting tough, but holy shit I was crying on the inside like a toddler in a grocery store throwing a temper tantrum because his momma won't buy him some skittles. Stay calm. How does it go, "woo sawwwww?"

Our supply guy was a grade-A dirt bag. He was short, white, beer gutted and sported dark, greasy, dandruff-infested hair that was always way out of regulations. A true embarrassment to the uniform, but every unit needed a supply guy and he was the card we were dealt. We called him Dog, because prior to morning PT one day back at Fort Lewis he was caught masturbating in his truck right in front of the troop area.

We believed he literally had to the IQ of a mentally handicapped person while holding a nervous stutter with a soft, high-pitched voice that often cracked. Or was that the innocent front ole Dog wanted us to see? He eventually got arrested for sending boxes of our equipment home to sell for cash. Yes, Dog stole and sold equipment we needed for war.

For the most part, we were able to salvage our own supplies. I told my guys to never expect anything while in a war zone. It's a war. Deal with the conditions given to you the best you can. Adapting to your environment is a big part of surviving in a hostile, foreign land. Some days we only had time to sleep, eat or get supplies. You had to choose just one.

I had to find a way to get some munchies before the cannibalism of my worst soldier began to seem like a good tactical idea. Perhaps a chubby one? Negative! Man up and find a way. As soldiers started filing thru to grab what they could, some turned to me with half a handful of food and offered me half of that.

"I don't need it. Eat that and go to sleep, brother. We're back out in 6 hours."

In my head, I imagined grabbing the minuscule portions offered and going at them like Cujo with rabies. I was too stubborn to take from my soldiers, which bordered lunacy. My eyes wandered around the area in desperation. Maybe I'll just smoke a Newport and that'll quench this hunger, which sadly worked from time to time. Not this time. Some food fell to the floor as I glared at the soldier who dropped it, then the food and then the soldier again. How could he do such a thing! That son of a bitch. *Woo sawwwww?*

My teeth began to ache. This was a new level of hunger for me. Even my teeth missed biting into something as cottonmouth set in. The area finally cleared. I was done acting like a patriarch. I about fell to my knees to scream, but didn't have the energy. As I took a deep breath and turned to attempt the Newport phenomenon I spotted something amazing. Someone had found an MRE and rat fucked the hell out of it. In their vampire-like lust for food, they had left something behind. Something magical.

A cookie. Not just an ordinary cookie, but a half-eaten M&M cookie. It looked majestic and I wanted it. I even looked around to see if anybody else was eyeballing it. Oh no, darling, its just you and me. I'm going in. As I reached down to swipe my "precious," I noticed a lot of other things. Why was there a plethora of wrappers and ammunition boxes underneath this cookie? Then the tunnel vision simmered and I realized it was lying near the top of a trash pile. I didn't give a damn. This was happening and I was eating the most glorious of meals straight out of a trashcan. That half-cookie left me stuffed and on cloud 9. I followed it up with that cigarette of victory to get a quick buzz to the head and pass out for a few.

I win this round, Iraq.

Kids are Your Friends... and Also Your Worst Nightmare

"The streets are empty," said Breastos in the front of the convoy with a trembling voice.

"Keep pushing," Pons responded from the rear.

Empty streets and an Iraqi police force that was literally running out of town, because they knew something unpleasant was about to go down is not how you want to start your day. These are clear signs of an ambush and that's what we got. It was an unwritten rule that if you saw kids playing in the street, chances are good that it's safe enough to travel thru. Just try not to run them over. They're like lap dogs that think they should run at the wheel of a 20-ton vehicle or stand under the ramp when you dismount to patrol.

"Mistah! Mistah! Bebsi, chocolate, watch!" ordered a random local kid.

"What? You're selling watches? Where did you get a watch to sell?" I asked

"Bebsi, chocolate, watch! GIVE ME!"

"Oh you want my watch... go play in traffic you little fucker."

"Fawckr?" Tilting his head to the side like a confused dog.

"Damnit."

First of all, "Bebsi," is supposed to be "Pepsi." A lot of people don't know this, but US forces actually introduced a lot of Iraqis' to the sound of "P" and although they have their own version in their alphabet now, many uneducated kids didn't get the memo and continued with "Bebsi!" Travesty. Coke is better anyways. How many fans did I just lose?

We felt safe with kids around, but they were merciless in their pursuit to annoy us into giving them freebees. White platoon didn't have much to give. I always wondered, "Who were the guys giving out Pepsi and chocolate and now apparently watches?" Maybe watches were just the evolution of their own greed. Ambitious. Good for you, kid.

We met with assets in safer neighborhoods and while the higher ups were inside for meetings, the rest of us doing outside security had to deal with the chee'rin. In an attempt to combat these little bastards and keep them at a less annoying distance we researched the nastiest of candies to give to them. SWEEDISH FISH. Ohhh yeah!

Ohhh no. Epic Fail.

Not only did they like these disgusting gelatin sweets, but they turned ravenous towards them. After a meeting, White mounted up on the Strykers and started rolling out. Guess who was en tow? You guessed correctly... Iraqi Lykens flying down the road at us. I swear they went down on all fours at some point.

"Just give them what they want!" I yelled.

"But I like these," Shmiddie sadly spoke.

"We'll be over run if you don't! Do it! I'll give you my chocolate MRE shake!"

"Really?"

Laughter followed of course, along with the children. Shmiddie tossed the bag of nasties to the urban piranhas. As the fish fell to the ground and were instantly covered in dust and grime, the kids picked them up and devoured the delicatessens. That can't be healthy, but we would live to see another day.

Sometimes we would have dance offs with the kids and other times we would teach them drinking songs, such as "Drunken Sailor." SFC Pons sang for them often.

"What do you do with a drunken sailor, what do you do with a drunken sailor, what do you do with a drunken sailor, early in the moooorning?!"

To which the local quartet or peanut gallery would reply...

"Do do do do doo do do, do do do do doo do do, do do do do doo do do, er-lie eh dah maaawningah!"

Close, but no dice.

As you can imagine it was a love/hate relationship from us to them. It was mostly a curious liking from them to us. Although they drove us nuts at some points, they also gave us indicators if something was out of the norm, because kids can't keep secrets and their nonverbal body language alerted us if there was trouble brewing or danger nearby. I met a lot of brave kids that led us to capturing enemies. I only hope there was no retribution against those kids from the enemies we didn't catch. I never grew numb to seeing dead kids or kids with blown off limbs simply because they were in the vicinity of Americans. Damn war... and damn Swedish fish.

The FOBbit:
An Expected Journey

"HEY!" I heard a man's voice yell in the night. I kept walking. "HEY!" Now I'm looking around, as it sounded closer. I see a tall E-6 with a crisp uniform walking my way, but as I turn to scowl at his tone, he stops. "Man, getchyo hands out yo pockets," he ordered.

I paused in curiosity before responding. Why was his uniform so clean and why did he smell so good from 50 feet away? It was the early winter of 2006 on FOB Falcon. It had been a bad day with multiple missions. It was bitter cold and windy. My entire body was crusted in sand and sweat with salt stains on my uniform. All I wanted to do was call home and talk about anything except war, but I couldn't. A few men at Falcon were killed and all communication was cut until the families were notified. This was called, "River City." Now I just wanted to get under some shelter and be left alone.

"EH! YOU HEAR ME?" he screamed again, only his voice cracking this time.

I just scowled then smiled and kept walking with my hands in my pockets. This guy went nuts, because I didn't follow his higher-ranking orders. I was hoping he would follow me back to my platoon area so he could ask SFC Pons about me. Pons would have told him to fuck off as we were getting ready for yet another mission. I couldn't believe I was talking to a FOBbit that had no idea what went on outside those walls and definitely had no idea what kind of person he was talking to. He just cried and whined as I kept walking with my hands warming inside my POCKETS.

Most FOBbits know they aren't doing anything exciting and keep to themselves. Other FOBbits just get the short end of the stick. People in combat arms are randomly selected to work in the TOC where someone is needed to work the radios for platoons on missions. I feel for those guys. They sign up for combat arms and then they're stuck answering radios and making coffee. I'm lucky to have been on the line my entire time deployed.

That pocket-protecting guy was a fueler NCO that didn't get out much and obviously didn't realize who was keeping him safe. Back in the states, or "garrison," we weren't permitted to put our hands in our pockets even during extreme weather. I agree it can look unprofessional, but in the middle of a war zone with a generation of soldiers that don't care about regulations and just want to serve their country? Fuck off! A FOBbit is someone that is in the military and deploys overseas, but is rarely in any danger as they stay on the FOB. You'll hear a lot of FOBbit's tell war stories and talk about their "PTSD." They're easy to spot. Just look for someone who's really proud, but you can't figure out why.

Face Raped

"Oh yeah, I see poison or venom in the middle there," one medic said.

"The dark shit in the middle? I see it alright," another medic announced.

"So how do you fix it?" I asked.

"Just don't touch it. Yeah... just don't touch it."

"You don't have *anything*, to help me out?"

"Let us know if it gets worse?"

"Wow."

White platoon was preparing to move from FOB Falcon to FOB Union III in central Baghdad in the spring of 2007. Temperatures were in the glorious 80's as we moved our equipment. Between runs to our new home, we had a few hours to eat and sleep so I crashed on the shrapnel proof matted and dusty floor of a Stryker. I bundled up some camouflage netting to use as a pillow.

A few hours later I woke and utilized the latrine. As I... wait, did I just say, "utilize the latrine?" Military lingo had finally set in. So... as I was washing my face, I noticed two tiny white dots right above my chin. They were very close together and I assumed they were new pimples, so I popped them both and rolled out. While in the green zone dropping off some wounded locals to medical facilities I kept asking Shmiddie the same question.

"What's the temperature?" I asked.

"For the hundredth fuckin' time food stamp, I don't know. What's wrong with you today?" he bickered back.

"I got the shakes man."

"There's no way you should be cold."

"I'm freezing."

All the way back to Falcon I was shaking in the gunner's hatch. I had no idea what was wrong with me. We parked our vehicles for a couple more hours of rest.

"What's on your face, Vance? Herpes of the mouth?" Puppet asked.

"Huh?" I responded quivering.

"There's a big ass red thing on your chin."

The two little pimples joined forces and started to swell. I felt a pulse on my damn chin and it started to burn. What the hell? I hadn't missed a single mission to injury or maintenance, so I just manned up and got ready to roll out again. White was set to roll for a third time that day by lining up at the gate and test firing our weapons. I had trouble seeing, my hands locked up like I had carpal tunnel and every single joint in my body began to ache. Standing up in the gunners hatch became an issue.

"Shmiddie, he's fucked!" our medic, Bullis, yelled from the inside of our Stryker while looking up at me.

"I'm good," I pathetically argued as I mean-mugged Bullis.

"Vance I don't even recognize your voice. Sometimes you just have to sit one out. We're dropping you off and you're going to go rest," Shmiddie ordered with perfect English.

"Roger," I was furious with myself.

I went back to my room, hit the mattress resting on a cot, bundled up and passed out. I didn't even hear White Platoon come back. I woke up 11 hours later thinking I had pissed my pants. It was sweat. I completely sweat thru the mattress. Disgusting.

"We'll get you checked out at Union III," Shmiddie affirmed as we prepped for a morning convoy north.

Half of my chin had been covered in this scab-looking crater with an extremely dark color in the shape of a cartoonish lightening bolt in the center. With the exception of the superhero symbol center, it resembled a nasty fever blister, or as Puppet dubbed it, "herpes of the mouth." To this day, I still have a zigzag scar just above the right side of my chin where the dark center was. We tried to find out how I got it when the light bulb went on above my head. That camouflage netting! We always found critters hiding in that thing. Some nasty spider crawled on my face and took a bite. I hope it crawled in my mouth and I ate it during my slumber. Bastard.

Rock Wall

"Kid Rock is going to be here tonight," Jonesy said.

"Yeah man, I hope we're back from mission in time to see 'em," I replied.

Our mission that night was to clear the train tracks of anything suspicious. Insurgents had been using the area between the tracks and the elevated route Jackson/Irish paralleling the walls of FOB Falcon to stage attacks and plant IED's. It was Christmas night and we wanted to get this done as quickly as possible to get back to see Kid Rock perform in the chow hall. We needed something to lift our spirits, so off we went into the night.

"White 4, this is White 2. We're stuck," SSG Breastos said over the net.

"2, 4. We just started 10 fucking minutes ago," SFC Pons.

"Roger."

We rolled out into our AO like three ducks in a row with our Strykers. Breastos' truck was in the front as they ventured into some murky ground. It was hard to tell if the ground in front of them would hold because of the different layers of nastiness. Human sewage would flow into any open area and mix with mud, giving the ground a greenish brown swirl that looked solid at night. Our lead Stryker drove right in and sank on its left side. Our dismounts jumped out as the trucks maneuvered into position to tow the lead Stryker. After trying several times with just one wench cable, we weren't making any progress. The Stryker kept sliding to its 9 o'clock.

"Grab a snickers bar gents," I said.

"Lets take the high ground and use two Strykers to pull 'em out," Shmiddie suggested. We were the kings of recovery.

I directed our truck towards Jackson/Irish and we attached our wench cable to the vehicle in despair. We were aligned to the stuck truck's 3 o'clock and prepared to be an anchor so it didn't sink any further while the rear truck attempted to pull from the 6 o'clock position.

If you know anything about wench cables then you know it takes a while to unwind them over 50 feet. It didn't help that our dismounts were trudging thru muddy sewage up to their knees. Merry fucking Christmas! As we were preparing the wenches, distant gunshots and explosions came closer. Pons called in air support since we were struggling in the winter conditions and weren't able to maneuver if a large enemy force decided to hit us.

"Shit!" hissed a soldier from the back right hatch after hearing a pop shot.

"You OK back there?" I asked from the gunner's hatch.

"I think a sniper just took a shot at us."

"If you can hear a sniper's shots, then you're not being shot at by a sniper."

"Good point."

Moments later two Apaches flew over to circle the area and scare off anyone thinking about taking advantage of our vulnerable position. They announced their arrival by launching red and green flares 75 feet above our heads to light up the sky.

"Wow! They fired Christmas colored flares for us!" Lemon rejoiced.

I didn't have the heart to say, "You fucking tard. Those are just random."

"Yeah man, Christmas colors for us."

We finally got the Stryker unstuck, but still had to complete the mission. For the next hour we carefully and slowly moved down the train tracks looking for evidence of enemy activity while avoiding another sticky situation. Finally we made it back to Falcon. Most of the platoon was covered in shit-mud as we shut down the trucks and hoped that Kid Rock was still performing for midnight chow. We weren't so lucky.

"He fuckin' killed it, man," Brown from Alpha troop stated.

"He's all done?" I asked with a glimmer of hope that he wasn't.

"Yeah. He was shit housed, but still put on a show for us. He even got a little emotional."

"Great."

We pathetically moved back to the old Iraqi barracks and crashed for the night, all the while wondering how awesome the performance was. It was still amazing Kid Rock took the time and flew into a dangerous area to perform for troops in dire need of a little entertainment. We were so close!

Famous people do USO tours all the time and its rare that you get an act that is mutually liked across the board such as Kid Rock. We also got a visit from a rapper I wasn't too excited about, but I was off mission and went to check it out anyways. He was in Baghdad to say "hi" and take pictures. That's more than I can say for most celebrities.

"Gonna go see Paul Wall, Vance?" D asked.

"Sure, why not," I answered.

It was late in our 15-month tour and we had the privilege of moving into the Green Zone for the last few months. Hello paradise and good living! We walked down to the coffee shop and waited in line as a member of Wall's entourage passed out pictures we could get signed. Yes, I still have it to this day. Don't judge.

One soldier had a fake dental grill and put it in to pose with Paul

Wall. He thought it would be a good idea since Paul Wall had colorful dental work as well. Wall just looked at the soldier like he was mental. It didn't help the soldier kept saying, "Yo! What it do?!" I kind of felt bad for Wall when dealing with fans like that. I had another approach when it was my turn to meet him.

"Hey, man," I said like a normal human being.

"How ya doin?" he asked.

"We all appreciate you coming all the way out here."

"No. I appreciate you all."

Wall looked me right in the eye with a straight face when he said that. It hit me that he really gave a shit and wasn't just doing this for a publicity stunt. I had a newfound respect for someone I had just met. Did I mention how surprised I was that I was taller than him? I was so happy I was taller than someone. Rappers all look so tall and tough when they're "pimpin' hoes" on TV. Bottom line is that Paul Wall was the real deal and his appearance gave us something to talk about for a day. The idea of home and not being able to go yet started to get to us.

Shoot the Medic...
Again... and Once More

"Vance, I want you to shoot me in the ass," Bullis asked.

"Shoot you in the ass with what?" I inquired.

"The non-lethal paintball gun."

"You realize if I miss your ass cheek and hit your asshole, its not going to be so non-lethal, right?"

"That's why I'm asking you to do it. I trust you."

"This is gonna to be hilarious."

Bullis was my platoon's medic and if I've learned anything in the military, it's that medics are crazy and very creative when it comes to killing boredom. Bodily harm is apparently not above them.

Every platoon was assigned a few paintball guns. These guns weren't like the ones you shoot at your buddies in the States. These paintball guns were shaped like Tommy Guns with a ten round disc that slipped right in front of the trigger. As a butt stock there was a CO2 tank that gave the paintballs a high velocity. In fact, these rounds came out of the short barrel at such a speed that if you hit someone in the eye it would go right into the brain and cause death. It didn't help that after 20 or 30 feet these rounds took nasty curves and could be highly inaccurate if you didn't practice first.

The rounds themselves were anything but circular. The rear of the paintball round was filled with yellow paint and had a flat bottom so you could stand the round up like a regular bullet shell. The front, or top, portion was dome shaped and filled with little metallic beads. These beads combined with a plastic shell and high velocity made for quite the violent strike. We were to use these in an attempt to reduce civilian deaths and win "hearts and minds." Hearts and minds was a crock of shit and was a good way to get US military members killed.

One day a vehicle was driving too fast for my comfort while my Stryker was in a blocking position nearby. I aimed for the driver's side door to warn the fucker to drive carefully around American forces. VBIEDs were a big threat. I fired. The round curved up and flew into the vehicle hitting the driver in the left shoulder. There was a huge yellow splatter as the round hit, covering his neck and head, so at first I thought I hit the guy in the ear and killed him. Luckily I just scared the snot out of him as he swerved, hit the curb and then got the hell out of Dodge thinking he got shot with an actual bullet.

Another local encounter with my girly Tommy gun was when an unsuspecting teenage boy was riding his bike too close to our position while on patrol. This was a time when suicide bike IED's were also a threat. Knowing this and being aware of my surroundings, I decided to give him a strong warning to go away. I put a paintball round right in the center of his handlebars. To give you an idea of how these paintball rounds freak people out, it caused the kid to completely flip his bike face forward. His entire torso and face were covered in yellow victory as we all had a laugh at his expense. This might seem cruel, but some Americans would have shot him with a real bullet thinking he was a suicide biker driving at that speed so close to our forces. Even his friends were laughing. That's what I call winning "hearts and minds."

Back to Bullis. He's a little over six feet tall, brown haired, well built with a face for modeling and he hales from a suburb of Boston.

Let me contest that while heavily intoxicated a thick Boston accent comes out of nowhere and I might as well be listening to fucking Chinese, because I needed a translator. Bullis walked about 30 feet away and bent over with his hind parts facing me. One of the guys walked behind me to film this exciting moment as I turned to the camera.

"What Bullis doesn't know is that I'm not that great of a shot," I whispered with a smile.

"What?!" Bullis hollered with his head between his legs.

"Nothin'! Stay down and look away, you!"

"The suspense is killing me."

Half the platoon was watching eagerly, grinning from ear to ear. As I took aim, I noticed a bulge in his right butt cheek. It had to be his wallet. It might be thick enough to sustain the pain. We've had our differences, but he was a dear friend and great drinking buddy back in the States so I had to hit that bulge to spare pain. The problem is that with this inaccurate weapon at that exact range, I have to play the curve perfectly. I wait for the breeze to die, exhale, hold steady and squeeze.

"*Poof!*" went the gun.

"Uhh!" went the Bullis.

I missed by about an inch to the right, but considering the weapon, it wasn't a bad shot at all. Bullis and I hugged it out as everyone laughed and cheered in the middle of our motor pool. It was a brief moment of entertainment and escape from our insane operational tempo of two to four missions a day for 15 months.

"How bad?" I asked.

"It stings," Bullis said with a frown and half smile.

Bullis was an outstanding and creative medic that I'm privileged to have seen in action. I always gave what little help I could, but on that day, he volunteered to be the butt of all jokes. Pun intended. On behalf of a lot of guys that needed a laugh we thank you Bullis. Can we go home now? No? Well then, we might as well shoot the medic one more time. Bullis went to the same spot, turned to face me and asked for it right in the abs. I didn't even let him finish his request when I raised the gun and immediately shot him. It left quite the welt... again. Bullis was a brave soul that surely couldn't keep raising the bar, right? Wrong.

"Bullis, you want us to shoot you with a non-lethal shotgun round?" asked Pons.

"How close and how bad will that hurt," Bullis asked.

"Oh it could actually kill you or castrate you, but only at a close range."

"OK, I'm going to run off the back of the Stryker and you can shoot me in the back."

We were pulling reconnaissance near the largest mosque under construction in Baghdad when our bored and brave medic wanted to end the boredom. I had already shot him twice with a non-lethal paintball round laced with miniature ball bearings, but Bullis wanted more pain for our entertainment. Who were we to stop such a dream from happening?

Pons was in the back left hatch and I was in the gunner's hatch as we communicated thru our headsets and Bullis got pumped up inside the Stryker.

"Hey Sergeant Pons, the first time you drop the ramp and he runs, just let him keep running to build up the suspense for a second run," I said.

"Hah! That's fucked up. I'm so going to do that," Pons responded.

"OK Mikey, drop the ramp," I told the driver.

"Run Bullis! *Chk chk!*" Pons yelled as he pretended to load a round in the chamber.

Bullis took off on a dead sprint into the middle of nowhere. He slowed down and looked back after 50 meters when we urged him to keep going, well out of accurate range. After 100 meters he realized the joke was on him. Bullis walked back to the truck.

"Sorry man, we had to do it!" Pons hollered as I laughed uncontrollably.

"Fuck you guys," Bullis gasped.

"Alright this time is for real."

Bullis took off at a slower pace the second time.

POW!

"Hoooo," Bullis howled as his body stiffened and he froze like a deformed statue.

He then tippy toed for a few steps before bending completely over. That didn't last long as that motion stretched his beaten skin. Bullis' entire backside from torso to heel was peppered with welts.

"I'm going to get fired," Pons said half scared and half laughing hysterically, "This shit is bananas, B.A.N.A.N.A.S, bananas!" Pons would sing and get that infectious Gwen Stefany song stuck in our heads after anything that got him excited.

When we turn to shooting the medic, repeatedly, it's time for this deployment to end.

Song Du Jour

I encountered all kinds of music from various comrades while serving. I got into country because it relaxed me. I got into heavy metal because the growling, longhaired and heavily pierced screamer that sounded like a constipated bear actually made sense to me in the middle of a firefight. Then there's music that nobody understands why I listen to it.

Crazyhorse Troop had been going balls to the wall for many months when we finally got a time to rest in the land known as "The Green Zone." Holy shit this place was awesome. People that were there for the duration of their time in Iraq had no idea how nice they had it. We got to stay in an old administrative building near the Ba'ath Party Headquarters on FOB Union III that was half collapsed in the middle from a bomb during the invasion. We stayed on the second floor where we spent downtime smoking cigarettes and playing the guitar. Occasionally we would be entertained by people running and screaming for shelter.

"What's that noise, Puppet?" I asked.

"I think it's an alarm for incoming," Puppet replied.

We never had the luxury of a warning before. We knew the incoming rounds weren't going to land on the FOB that day, because we didn't hear the whistle the rounds make if they are close. However, the people who never went outside the wire sure as hell didn't know that. They were screaming and scurrying like scared squirrels to find a hard shelter while dawning green helmets and black protective vests. They had no idea where they were going, but it was fascinating to see people freak out when the danger was so far off.

"The fuck are they doing, Vance?" Puppet asked while snickering.

"I can't breathe!" I laughed.

You'll have to forgive us for being so desensitized. Actually, don't. Just get used to it. Our tempo slowed to just two missions or patrols a day and spending a week at a time at C.O.P. (Combat Outpost) Remagen on Haifa Street then going back to missions for a couple more weeks. After missions we would go to the open area on the first floor created by the invasion's blast. There was a local guy that was allowed to come in, set up a kabob stand and sell cheap food to some stinky soldiers. We simply referred to the area as "The Hodgy Stand." The local guy also set up a small tube TV with a Jerry-rigged antenna that would make even MacGyver proud.

The TV in the Hodgy Stand would only show 3 channels. One was news in Arabic. Another was an Arabic music video station. The third showed American music videos. The thing about that channel is it showed the same three videos all-day, everyday. So after mission we would run to the Hodgy Stand to eat kabobs, drink stale "Bebsi" from tiny 8 oz. cans, smoke and watch these videos to relax, but what was so special about these videos?

Before I reveal these videos I feel the need to ask you to imagine our mindset. It was the summer of 2007, we hadn't seen a real female since the previous summer and we stunk like shit. We smelled so bad that we could be walking and as the wind picked up from 300 meters away, stop dead in our tracks, simultaneously turn and BAM!

"Chicks dude. I smell chicks."

At the Hodgy Stand we sat in awe as Rihanna's "Umbrella," Avril Lavigne's "Girlfriend," and Fergie's "Big Girls Don't Cry," echoed throughout the accidental courtyard. White Platoon found an escape. These songs brought us such happiness that we were there almost everyday. Rihanna was in sparkling silver body paint sounding like a stuttering badass with her "ella, ella, ella, eh, eh, oh." Avril was running around in a schoolgirl outfit being chased by a hotter version of herself. Fergie was rockin' tight jeans and a pouty face while leaving her man. That's right, Fergie, leave that asshole and find a better man. I'm single. Just saying. No? That's cool.

Those videos created a memory of my brothers just relaxing in a world of madness. It was a time where we weren't being shot at, blown up, found screaming obscenities at each other and the higher ups left us alone. It was peace during war. Memories like this one help all of us deal with the bad ones. Whenever I hear those three songs come on the radio you can bet everything on me turning it up as loud as I possibly can and smiling for the duration and giving absolutely zero fucks who sees me doing it.

September had come in 2007 and we were on our way home to a popular tune that was fitting... Green Day's, "Wake me up, when September ends." A bittersweet ending to a long deployment. Hello America! I wonder how we'll be received.

HOMEBOUND

I was so excited to get home and spend time enjoying my first full day off in over a year with Americans. A couple of buddies and I had a trip planned to Australia. I was headed off to tryout for a military soccer team that traveled the world and if that backfired I was going to drop the SF packet I prepared while overseas. Things were looking up and I couldn't be happier or more relaxed. I would learn that coming home was like a mission in a warzone... nothing goes as planned.

Hippies Throw Oranges?

"At least it's not like Vietnam and everyone supports the troops."

"Oh look at you, living in your tiny bubble."

I received mixed reactions from different groups of people in my life when I enlisted. My family didn't quite know how to react and usually just asked if I was sure I wanted to commit to something like that. Most of my friends were the same way since not too many of them joined the service. A lot of people were just curiously excited to know someone about to go to a once-in-a-generation type of war. One irate female cussed me out in front of a restaurant full of people.

"So hey guys, I decided to enlist over spring break," I mentioned.

"Are you a fucking idiot?!" a girl yelled as she stood up at the table.

"Probably?"

"Did you at least sign up to be an officer?"

"Nope."

I definitely didn't see that reaction coming. It was my first encounter with a strongly opinionated person that wasn't fond of the idea of war. I let her vent and feel good about herself and then quietly left. The things that people say about events that are set in motion won't matter in the long run. Ultimately that girl was the actual "fucking idiot" for attempting to humiliate a guy that just wanted to go on an adventure helping a country that couldn't help itself. There's nothing wrong with voicing an opinion, but for God's sake at least find out why somebody enlisted before assuming they did it in the name of killing babies.

Off I went into the military and to Fort Lewis. Hello west coast. On the weekends we would do anything to get out of the barracks. Along the I-5 corridor, the three major cities for "Joes" to go to party at are Seattle, Tacoma and Olympia. Tacoma was the closest place to base and although the locals loathed our primitive behavior, we supplied a lot of money to their economy, so they put up with us better than most citites. Seattle was 45 minutes north and far enough away that people maintained a "support the troops" attitude, but it was close enough so that college boys recognized our hair cuts and stayed out of our way when talking to college ladies. Olympia was another story.

"You're in the service aren't ya, boy," an old man grumbled with a sneer.

"Yes, sir," I replied with a smile.

"Then fuck you! Fuck all you baby killers!"

I was in shock. Then I was angry. Real angry. Olympia, for the most part, was home of the hippies. They didn't care what your reasons were for joining or what was really going on overseas. They just wanted somebody to hate. Our haircuts easily gave us away in a city where musicians and white Rastafarians roamed the streets. Some bars solely existed for political gatherings. That old man at the bar almost got pummeled, but we decided to walk it off to the next bar. From that night on we tried avoiding places of that nature.

Now, after my first deployment, our Strykers were loaded onto huge ships and we flew home, except a small contingent of soldiers that stayed with the Strykers for security thru pirate-infested waters. The ship arrived about a month later at one of our local ports in Washington State. We notified the public the ships were arriving at a different port than the actual destination to avoid a hippy gathering. It wasn't long before they figured it out.

The first wave of Strykers were off the boat and ready to convoy back to Fort Lewis. Police officers were at the gates of the port to both escort us while on the highway and keep the hippies back. The hippie's numbers swelled. I was in the second chalk (convoy) and watched as the first chalk took off.

"These assholes are throwing oranges at us!" one soldier said.

"Oranges?" I asked.

"Yeah, who the fuck throws oranges?"

"That's gotta hurt. There's nothing peaceful about being hit with an orange. What kind of hippies are these?"

As the first chalk continued thru the gates, a hippy driving a car decided he was going to ram a Stryker with his Pinto sized vehicle. This was funny because that hippy didn't realize a Stryker was 20 tons until he was just meters away and changed his mind, slamming his brakes. I definitely thought hippies were peaceful people. Throwing heavy softball size fruit and trying to ram us with cars was a lot different than flowers in your hair. What would they do next?

One hippy actually pulled a Tie Neman Square by lying down flat in the middle of the road in an attempt to stop the convoy and allow further fruit attacks on us. What that hippy didn't know is that there is easily two feet of clearance under a Stryker and we could simply drive over them without causing any bodily harm.

"We got one lying down up here. Want me to just run her over since we ain't gonna actually touch her?" said the lead vehicle.

"Nah, cause then she'll sit up as we're rolling over her and I don't wanna clean that mess up. We just got these washed," said the convoy commander.

"Roger."

It was time for my chalk to start its move. The gates to the port were pretty far away and we couldn't see what was going on, so for all we knew we were about to get an orange barrage to the face. Instead we got a nice surprise from the local police force. They were armed with paintball guns (not like ours) and sprayed the out of control group of anti-military hippies. By the time my Stryker made it thru the gates, the hippies were doused in multi-color paint splatters resembling a tie-die design, holding hands and flipping us the peace sign. Finally, a stereotypical hippy move! We laughed and waved to the police as they waved back and cheered us on.

"Mat, why don't you ever fight back when people act so rudely about something they know nothing about?"

People ask me this all the time. If I fought back it would ruin everything I believe in about being a soldier. I've had things hurled at me, been cussed at, spat at and threatened on many levels, but I've not yet raised a hand at the people that disrespect us. Many years from now nobody will remember what the hippies did, but they sure as hell will remember what soldiers did in a time of war. Perhaps one day I will fight back and I feel sorry for the family of the person on the receiving end of that, but for now I can only smile and walk away from people that will never understand what soldiers really do. This way they look like fools in the eyes of anyone watching.

Coming home was already not what I thought it would be.

Mili-Caring

"Dude, I thought you went in to get a cavity taken care of?" Walker asked.

"I did," replied Wombley.

"Then why are your front four teeth missing?"

"I don't know! They put me under and I woke up to this."

Poor Wombley was one of many victims to terrible physicians during basic training. It would inspire me to never go to a military dentist and keep extremely good care of my teeth. It's bad enough that while growing up, we all view a dentist's office as a torture chamber. Imagine going in for a simple procedure and you wake up to four of your pearly whites missing in action.

"Sergeant Vance, I want you to take this black sharpie, circle the non-surgical knee and then make an "X" inside the circle so the surgeons know which knee not to operate on," the nurse said.

"Are... are you kidding me?" I asked with eyes wide.

"It happens."

In late 2007, after my first deployment, a friendly game of flag football turned into tackle. I was still in the shape of my life when a freak accident left my torso turned in one direction and my right foot stuck into the turf facing 180 degrees in the opposite direction. Most people "tear" their ACL. I snapped mine completely in half, leaving nothing but two nubs on the inside of my right knee.

"Try to walk it off Vance," Nystrom said.

"Something's not right," I hissed.

"Don't get up, man. I heard the pop from the other side of the field," Jackson said.

It would be a long road to recovery and a path that would lead me to despise military doctors. After hobbling around for almost two months, a spot for surgery opened up at the base hospital in early 2008. During those two months I limped around Australia and said goodbye to my dreams of professional soccer. The way things were going I kissed my SF chances adios as well.

A quick snip about that base hospital... the best equipment and the worst staff. When I originally went to the ER they told me I had a sprained knee and wrapped it tightly with a soft cast. Not only a mis-diagnosis, but the worst thing you can do to a knee with my injury is apply heat. I didn't sleep much that night and all they had to do was give me an MRI, but that was "too expensive" to do at the time.

After I circled my good knee during pre-surgery I hopped onto a mobile bed for the procedure and got hooked up to an IV to knock me out. As the drugs began to take a hold on my body I began to shake. The hospital staff rolled me into the operating room. This isn't something I wanted to be awake for. As the bed came to a halt, I looked around the room and saw all kinds of shiny tools they were going to use on me as well as lots of people with masks on. This made me uneasy.

"Oh shit, he's still not under," a male nurse said to the female nurse.

"High tolerance maybe. Up the dose," the female replied.

"Why am I shaking?" I asked.

"Count to 100."

"Wooooooooooon, choooooooo, teeeeee," yep, time to go night nights.

Hours later...

"Sergeant Vance, are you with me?" a nurse asked.

"What time is it?" I asked.

"For the tenth time its about 2:30."

"I just woke up, how did I ask nine other times?"

"You've been awake for 10 minutes repeating that question and now you're actually aware of yourself."

"Oh, sorry."

"Don't be, it's been hilarious. Go ahead and pee in this jar."

"I don't have to piss."

"You will when you stand up."

The post-operation room is where the comedy is. We've all seen the videos on YouTube where a kid comes out of surgery and is saying wacky things on the car ride home. Now imagine a bunch of crazed veterans. Apparently I behaved and just wanted to know what time it was since I had asked Sanchez and Jonesy to pick me up. Pretty damn cognoscente for a doped up guy if I do say so myself. They walked into the room as I went to sit up.

"Oh man, I gotta piss bad," I muttered.

"Told ya. I have things to do so your buddies will have to assist you," said the old lady nurse.

Sanchez looked confused and Jonesy started laughing.

"What she mean, 'assist you,' Vance?" Sanchez asked.

"I still can't feel much so somebody has to hold me up and the other has to... hold the plastic jar while I... urinate."

"I'll hold him," Sanchez snapped and immediately took the easy job.

"Hey, hey Jonesy," I said with a wink.

"Fuck you, Sanchez," Jonesy whispered while laughing.

Sanchez stood behind me, held me up and looked away while

Jonesy stood in front of me while I relieved myself.

"You owe me a lot of drinks, Vance," Jonesy said.

"Yup-p-p-p-p," I tried to respond, but the drugs still had a firm grasp on my mind.

Something went wrong during the course of the surgery and the doctor who operated on me failed to pass a referral on to my rehabilitation office because apparently she was too excited to go on vacation. The problem with that is the rehab place won't accept me until the operating doctor sends a referral and she wasn't reachable. So what happens to Mat? My knee locks at 90 degrees for over a week and rehab was supposed to begin three days post-op.

I plea my case with documents to another rehab place on base and they accept me. No progress with bending the knee after another week. Doctor Ditz comes back and I'm ready to go on a rampage. She admits her error, but the damage is done and you can't just sue the military. Ditz calls me to come in for a procedure known as a "manipulation."

"You'll come in, we'll put you under and make your knee bend," she assured me over the phone.

I show up to the hospital the next day.

"Here's a pillow," Ditz said.

"What's this for?" I asked

"You're going to want to put your face in this. We won't be putting you under."

"That's not what you told me last night."

"This way is more convenient for us and saves money. We're going to give you an epidural then force the knee to bend while you're awake."

"Epi-what?"

"It's what we give pregnant women during the birthing process."

"Riiiiiight. Lets get on with it then."

I put my face in the pillow, felt some pressure in my back and then what felt like a cool liquid going down my spine. Two male doctors came up and Ditz directed them to my lower leg. She looked uncertain of what was about to happen. I just glared at her as if to say, "You better unfuck this situation, bitch." All three grabbed my right shin, lifted my leg and begin to slowly try to bend it.

"Ummm, errrr, yeah I can feel that," I mentioned with a grimace.

"Give him more," Ditz ordered more numbing agent.

They took a break to let the drugs set in and ten minutes later we went again. Same result. Repeat. Now I was numb. They put all the force they could into bending my knee and it started to move. I heard the scar tissue and cartilage breaking up inside my knee, but felt no pain... yet. After the three stooges were done with their manipulation that put saving money over a patient's comfort, I was wheeled into a holding area because they forgot to get me a room. This keeps getting better and better.

My leg was placed in a machine that would keep it constantly in motion, thus making sure it wouldn't get stuck at 90 degrees again. While I was looking at this contraption a pretty female nurse came up to me with some kind of rubber sack and a tube. Our eyes met and she looked surprised.

"You're awake?" she asked.

"They gave me a pillow?" I smiled.

"I was going to insert this catheter."

"Well I still can't feel anything below the waist."

"You won't feel weird by me doing this while you're awake?"

"I don't give a shit about anything anymore. Just don't judge me because I don't know what's going on down there right now."

"Ha! I would never."

She inserted the catheter and I was finally wheeled off to a room. I was on a morphine drip at the time. In order to be released, the hospital had to verify that I would feel minimal pain without morphine so they would periodically wean me off. The first time was the worst. The hospital staff didn't tell me. I started to feel a pulse in my knee and started clicking my morphine button to no avail. Within 30 minutes I was screaming bloody murder while clinching to the rails on the side of my bed like a patient in a psych ward on level 8 of the hospital.

It was the worst pain I had ever felt in my life and still to this day. To make matters worse, a captain with three interns walked into my room unannounced not knowing what kind of pain I was in. He wanted to show them the results of the manipulation by grabbing my leg and moving it in places it wasn't ready to go.

"Gentlemen, as you can see..." he began.

"AHHHH! Put my leg down you stupid son of a bitch! Get the fuck out! GET! THE! FUCK! OUT!" I interrupted in surround sound.

"What's going on in here?!" a nurse came to the rescue as the captain and his cronies ran out.

She took one look at me in tears, red faced, veins bulging from the neck, grabbing my knee and then pursued the captain to cuss him out. At the time I didn't even know he outranked me by quite a bit, but sometimes you have to put rank aside and humble somebody. He later called to apologize and didn't have the testicular fortitude to do it in person. I just hung up on him.

I then got news that my Grandma passed away and I couldn't get home for the funeral at Arlington National Cemetery. My time in the states continued to get worse. Send me back to fucking Iraq already. The rest of the time in the hospital was a daze. I don't even remember some of my chain of command coming in to check on me. My hospital gown had folded up and my privates were out in the open.

"Yeah, you're balls were definitely showing," my lieutenant, Jamal said.

"Don't remember that," I said shaking my head.

"You were like, 'HEY!' all happy to see us."

After a few days the hospital decided they needed more space. They pulled the catheter and sent me home with a similar concoction that accidently killed Heath Ledger that same year. I even had morphine pills. Who the hell gives a single guy that lives in the barracks morphine to play with? I was in and out of the hospital and don't remember anything from the first half of 2008. I'm not a fan of hospitals as you can imagine. They hold some of the best people in the world, yet they also possess some of the biggest airheads. It's a crapshoot so good luck and watch your back out there people!

It was time to be with my brothers and cheer up. They tend to go to great lengths to accomplish this and I love them for it. Tomorrow's a new day...

Tongue Chicken

They have no shame. They don't crack under pressure. They are fractionally psychotic. They are crazy people that I trust with my life. I could never do what they do. What group am I talking about? Combat Medics. Corpsmen. PJ's.

Early on in my service, I broke down the different jobs in my squadron to describe to my civilian friends who asked, "What are scouts like?" or "What are infantrymen like" or "What are counter intelligence guys like." Infantrymen are simple and like to smash things much like a bull in a china shop. Scouts are curious creatures that smile if you say, "Whatever you do, don't push that button" and then they push the hell out of that button. CI guys had to be chameleons, because there was only one per platoon. They weren't trained to be grunts, but had to start acting like they were. Then there were the medics.

"Hey Vance, we're all hanging out on the first floor if you wanna drink," Trezza proclaimed.

"Sounds like fun, man. Be down in a few," I replied.

In early 2005 I had just finished initiation when things started to calm down... or would they? I only knew the medics of Crazyhorse and I was en route to meet many more throughout the squadron. Up until that point I had only heard rumors of medic shenanigans and was quite curious, as a good scout should be.

I walked downstairs to the first floor of the barracks and took a left down the narrow cinder block hallway. I could already hear a raucous. I knocked on the first door to the right with a beer in hand.

"Come in!" someone yelled.

Thru the door I went into a bloody massacre. There were medics working in pairs giving each other IV bags of saline while drinking heavily and smoking cigarettes. I looked to my left into a latrine with white tile flooring covered in blood splatter. Back to my front a medic was standing ready with a stopwatch.

"Alright! Ready! Go!" he yelled.

Not only were they giving each other IV's, but they were seeing who could do it the fastest. This was impressive for the successful ones, but for everyone else, blood dripped to the floor and sometimes squirted thru the air. My eyes were wide open.

"7.2 seconds!" a medic with a stopwatch announced one of the times. "Wanna try one, Vance?"

"Um, nah, I'm good," I said.

Everyone shouted and drank as blood flowed well into the night. These guys don't mess around. Even when they drank they found ways to be better medics.

Medics had to be the jokesters in most situations, because they didn't have much to do unless somebody was wounded. Grab-ass would be their clear field of expertise. Most combat arms soldiers were always trying to prove how tough or manly they were. Medics loved to exploit this. For instance if two soldiers were grappling on the ground, a medic would encourage them to pick it up a notch to declare a winner.

"Check his oil!" one would yell.

"Check his oil?" I asked.

"Yeah man, shove your thumb up his ass! Establish male dominance! Trust me, he'll give up!"

"I'm so glad I'm not grappling right now."

Medics would also take advantage of a soldier talking trash while inebriated. If that soldier claimed he could beat anyone at anything, a medic went to the go-to game of Tongue Chicken. The game started with two completely heterosexual males standing a few feet apart. Then both would be told to stick their tongues out and start moving towards each other. The first one to bail out would lose. In most cases the soldier would bow out immediately at the thought of French kissing another dude. However, "tough guys" had to be taught a lesson.

One night in 2008 at my Tacoma townhouse off 38th Street, a bunch of us were participating in "Fifth Night." On Fifth Night, nobody could leave for the bars until everyone finished a fifth of their choice of liquor. Towards the end of everyone's bottle the trash talking commenced.

"I can take you at tongue chicken, Bullis," JD threatened.

"I don't think you can," Bullis responded nonchalantly.

"Only one way to find out."

I was sitting on my decrepit futon right next to JD as the words spewed out while Bullis was standing in front of us. Bullis then stuck his tongue out.

"Aw shit, here we go," I whined.

JD followed suit with his tongue, but remained seated as Bullis walked up and jumped on his lap, straddling him. Tongues are still out people. Bullis gave JD a chance to get out by briefly pausing, but JD was so drunk he could barely hold his eyes open, much less know a 200 lb man was on his lap. In went the medic and tongues touched. We all took pictures and laughed our asses off. JD still had no idea he was making out with a man. When his eyes opened, he turned away.

"I win!" Bullis announced.

"Did that just happen?" JD asked.

"Your girlfriend is gonna be so pissed," I replied. "And Bullis, you're the gayest straight guy I know."

Laughter followed as we headed off to the bars piggy backing my crippled ass past drunken bouncers that loved us. Never threaten a medic folks, especially if you're a heterosexual male. You lose every time. This group was making me feel better already and I could almost start walking without a limp.

The Amazing Racists

"1, 2, 3, White!" our platoon yelled on the football field.

"Power!" E followed with a holler and we all laughed.

E isn't a white guy and our platoon isn't called "White" because of any ethnic backgrounds. You become so close with members of your platoon that the differences amongst you are poked at in brotherly love, not in hate like racism. Our diversity makes us better. From the outside, I can see how we all seem like bigots, but I believe a true bond is when you can say whatever is on your mind and only the person you're talking to can judge whether or not you're serious.

For instance, Jonesy is from the small Indiana town of Terre Haute. Sanchez is from Nicaragua and came to the states around the age of 10. Terre Haute is a predominantly white town and Sanchez is from an entirely different country made up of mostly Hispanic people.

"I never even seen a black person 'til I went to college and my roommate was on the basketball team," Jonesy would say.

Jonesy and Sanchez have one of those bonds where they can say whatever they want to each other, no matter how offensive it sounds to the rest of the world. I should say Jonesy could say whatever he wanted to. It's not Sanchez's style to say anything back that might even sound offensive to any listeners.

"Hey, you goin' out tonight? Hey, spic, I'm talking to you," Jonesy would instigate.

"Ha-ha, you funny Jones," Sanchez laughed then his face went to a serious look as the rest of us laughed harder.

They were roommates in the barracks and they knew everything there is to know about each other. It's the reason that kind of language can only be shared between the two of them. Sanchez knows Jonesy is from a part of the country where people say racist things, but Jonesy himself was no such man. He was all about jokes and having a good time. Just to cheer Sanchez up, Jonesy would pop off at him, instantly cracking him up along with the rest of us.

"You're going out with us tonight and you don't have a choice," said Jonesy.

"Oh yeah?" Sanchez curiously responded. "How you gonna do that?"

"Just cause I said so, wetback."

"Hahaha that's a racist thing to say to a Mexican, not a Nicaraguan."

"You're all the same, ain't ya?"

"Fuck you, Jonesy, I came here on a boat."

Sound terrible? Then you've never had a bond with someone willing to give there life for yours and you really need to lighten up because this story only gets more intense from here.

"Cracka," Taser said to his white friend.

"Spic," Neirbo returned.

"Uh, huh, huh, huh," they both chuckled quietly.

Taser and Neirbo were in Raider platoon together and went thru a lot. They would do anything for each other at a moment's notice. That doesn't change the fact that they loved to remind each other of what race they were in the most vulgar manner. Few people can relate to this kind of friendship. Especially intoxicated people that overheard them at a bar.

"Eh, what did you just call him?" asked a Hispanic man turning around from the bar.

"I called my friend a spic. Don't worry about it," Neirbo bluntly told the man.

"Oh, well I am worried about."

"I'm the last dude you want to fuck with."

Neirbo did the right thing and just walked outside to have a smoke. He really was the last person anyone wanted to get into a tiff with. Neirbo is a ginormous individual standing 6'5" and 265 pounds of all muscle. The disgruntled man at the bar was about 5'8," 175 pounds and suffering from "Little Man Syndrome" or LMS. People with LMS are tired of not being noticed and when someone like Neirbo walks into the same room as them. They feel the need to prove their toughness. I call these people, "Tough Guys." Neirbo and Taser came back inside and stood near the same location with the rest of us, including our friend Hurricane.

"Weak ass muthafuckas," LMS said under his breathe while mean mugging everyone.

"It's not a good idea to fuck with my large friend," Hurricane told LMS.

"He won't kill me. I'll kill him."

Well that wasn't very nice.

Things seemed to calm down for a while when Holly, Hurricane's girlfriend who worked at the bar, spotted ole LMS sneaking behind the bar. He grabbed an ice pick and turned to go towards Neirbo. Holly and another coworker tried to stop LMS and told him to leave, but he pushed both women down a couple of stairs leading to the icebox. Hurricane saw this and went to the rescue. I was at a bar table talking to a lovely lady friend when I saw this all happen. I could barely walk without crutches at the time so I made an executive decision to make sure we won this battle.

"NEIRBO!" I yelled.

Sucks to be LMS on this night. Neirbo turned as I motioned towards Hurricane and seven others from our group ran towards the action. Hurricane managed to shove LMS out the back door of the bar and into the alley. LMS had a couple of buddies follow, not knowing seven of Hurricane's friends were on the way. They made a poor decision to gang up on our guy. A brawl ensued out back that left LMS and his friends hospitalized.

"I'm afraid its time to go," I said to my lady friend.

"Meet at your place?" she insisted.

"Sounds good. Now I'm going to round up as many as I can before the cops arrive."

Everyone made a run for it as I hobbled to my car to do what little a crippled guy could do in a bar brawl and offer an escape vehicle. Great success. LMS and company weren't so lucky. Not only did they get hospitalized with fractured skulls, but I'm sure the police had a good laugh when they decided they wanted to press charges. Bar surveillance cameras caught the entire episode and clearly our group acted in self-defense from a crazy person with an ice pick that hits women.

All of it could have been avoided if LMS had minded his own business. People can be too sensitive. A simple conversation between two friends having a good time turned into a bloodbath. And why? Because an individual didn't know the context of a few comments. Were racial slurs used? Yes. Does it mean they were used in a hateful manner and everyone should be up in arms? No.

So, are we racists? No, we just have an amazing bond shared by few. But if you're content on passing judgment we'll go along with it to mock your sensitivity and deem ourselves, "The Amazing Racists." In the words of Matty Mayhem, "I SAID, GOOD DAY!"

My knee was healing and I was anxious to get back to work after many nights of debauchery with my brothers. My spirits were on the up and I was excited to be an NCO again.

Meat Gazer

"We got a squatter!" I announced brazenly from the latrine.

"Ohhhhh!" responded the long line of Crazyhorse men waiting to take a piss test.

During a urinalysis to test for illegal drug abuse in the ranks, there is one soldier that documents everything and has to take a class in order to be in that position. Another soldier is picked at random to be the meat gazer. That lucky soldier was responsible for going into the latrine with each soldier and watching him urinate to verify that the piss in the cup was indeed his own. Oh my.

When I was selected to be the meat gazer I would turn it into a show, because if I had to do a disturbing duty I might as well have fun with it. Some guys would get nervous pissing in front of another man and we dubbed that fear "stage fright." If a soldier had stage fright we would make them drink copious amounts of water until they couldn't hold their urine any longer. That tactic never made sense to me, as I'm sure it diluted any trace of drugs. To help some friends that had substance abuse problems, I just kept quiet about that theory as long as they could perform their job.

Some soldiers would just need some help urinating and no, I'm not talking about physically helping them down below, you pervert. Simply turning on the sink and talking about waterfalls would do the trick. With other soldiers I would stand about two inches behind them.

"How ya doin' there, buddy?" I'd awkwardly ask.

"Oh fuck off, man," they'd all reply.

"Everything going OK *down* there?"

"I hate you right now."

To mess with them even more I would wait until I heard them pissing and then start massaging their shoulders. Since they were in the act of filling the cup, they couldn't turn to punch me, so it was funny to see them squirm and freak out. To civilians this seems creepy, but to those of us watching in line it was pure entertainment. Every now and then we would have a special case. A soldier would turn to me with dreaded verbiage.

"Sergeant Vance, I have to go number two," a soldier said.

"You motherfucker," I responded with dead eyes.

"So what do we do?"

"*You* will sit your ass on the toilet and *I* will grab a chair and sit down right in front of you in the stall."

"What?"

"Oh yeah, it's on. You don't get off that easy. Have fun filling that cup with piss while you're trying to drop a deuce."

A soldier that had to go poo would be deemed a "squatter." It could be an innocent coincidence or it might be an attempt to be in private to swap another soldiers urine sample with your own. The trick for me was making people feel uncomfortable. I never had to literally check out somebody doing their business. I was just boisterous and close enough to deter them from trying to cheat the system or putting me in a shitty spot to either report them or do something my superiors wouldn't approve of. Finding a spot on the wall just over their shoulders was my point of focus.

The things soldiers have to do in the military isn't quite what you thought now is it? No worries, because many of us would rather not enlighten the world of certain duties such as being a meat gazer. I, on the other hand, don't give a shit. I just want to be as accurate as possible so you know exactly what you're in for if you join. Also, this will open your eyes on what to expect with that veteran you may have just started dating... ha! We're all a little loopy, but that's ok. Even you have issues.

Training was getting old. Drinking was our escape. Meat gazing was fun for everyone. It must be time to deploy again. My leg was close enough to normal and I was excited to see the new group of FNG's perform overseas.

NUMBER 2

With my knee in shambles and nothing going for me that I had planned for, I took a long look at my platoon in late 2008. I wasn't too fond of some people that outranked me, but the men I had trained over the past year were outstanding soldiers. They made me proud to be their NCO. Even when I was awful to them, they stood by my side. I couldn't watch them leave for war without me. I re-enlisted for 2 more years after my initial 4-year time was over. I took the oath on an Oregon beach while training in front of only my platoon. I was then tossed into the cold Pacific Ocean in celebration. I walked up to my men and told them I did this for them. Little did we know, the next year of our lives would be the biggest mind-fuck of all time and arguably the longest year of my life.

Burn Toppy Burn

There was this guy... we'll call him Lieutenant Birdbrain. He was our Platoon Leader. Sad face.

"Alright White Platoon, lets see if you're smarter than a 10 year old," I said on the net while we were pulling security for engineers late one night at a new checkpoint we would soon be living at for days at a time.

Friends and family had mailed a card game during my second deployment that asked questions at an elementary school level.

"First question; do astronauts travel faster or slower than 18,000 mph while in space?" I asked while imitating a baseball commentator's voice.

"That's easy, way faster," Birdbrain proclaimed.

"You sure?" asked Courtney.

"Yeah, astronauts come back from space younger than when they left Earth."

"And how is that, sir?"

"Because they are traveling at the speed of light; way faster than 18,000 mph."

Of course the entire truck pretended to laugh at his stupid joke, but then we realized something. Birdbrain was serious! Then the entire truck legitimately burst into laughter.

"So, you're telling me that we have achieved warp speed?" Courtney asked.

"Well, yeah. What?"

"Did they teach you that at West Point, sir?"

"So here's the next question," I changed the subject to prevent our heads from exploding.

I came across some real characters during my military time, but rarely did I see this level of turd in a leadership position. Birdbrain was the highest-ranking person in our platoon. Back at Lewis in 2009, the first word we got about him was that he was a tactical and social failure.

"Oh your platoon is getting Birdbrain?" said another LT that graduated from West Point with him.

"Why do you say it like that?" I asked.

"Well everyone except for him passed the last set of exercises."

"Is he going to be difficult to work with?"

The LT just smiled and walked away. Oh boy. We're getting ready to deploy in a few months and we've got a piece of work on the way.

"Bet you wish you took that promotion last year, Sergeant Vance, *ah-hehehe*," Our new platoon sergeant, SFC Rasp, stated with a flem-filled throat.

"Not really, I love being a team leader."

"But as the team leader in alpha section, you're on the LT's truck. You get to fix 'em."

"Well... shit, fuck, damn."

It was a shame we had to switch LT's so close to deploying. Our previous one, Jamal Khan, was outstanding. He was born in the United Arab Emirates, graduated from Michigan State, average height and build, black hair, brown eyes, great sense of humor and was of the Muslim faith. Jamal's humor, thick skin and faith produced non-PC jokes throughout the platoon, which eased tensions during a time when some people weren't very excepting of Muslims. It also allowed a lot of our guys to ease into a culture many of us were naïve to. Myself included. Socially, he was the perfect LT. If he saw something wrong with a platoon member, he would ask that soldier's first line supervisor if that was normal behavior. If it wasn't, the first line would correct that soldier. To say that my second deployment would have been better with Jamal is a serious understatement.

"Sergeant Vance, the new LT is here," Rasp gurgled.

"Clear your fucking throat," I whispered to myself.

"Huh?"

"On the way, sergeant!"

I walked into our platoon cage where I saw a kid of average height, thin, pale, brown haired and nervous.

"Hi guys, I'm Lieutenant Birdbrain. I just want to start off by saying everyone has said I have an easy job to fill, because I'm walking into a platoon that knows their shit. That being said, I want you to know that I know I have a lot to learn from you all. I'm not going to get in your way. Just do your thing."

The next year and a half would make this statement erroneous.

"What do you think, Vance?" someone asked.

"Seemed like a rehearsed speech and he gives off this... douche bag aura," I said, "but time will tell."

During our first field exercise in Yakima with Birdbrain we were told not to use cell phones by the squadron commander, a Lieutenant Colonel and very high-ranking man. Of course, we would use our cells any way, but Birdnuts took it one step further. He aimlessly walked out in the open in broad daylight looking like the Verizon guy who always annoyingly asked "Can you hear me now?" We could see our troop commander staring him down from a half mile away. They would have a one-sided conversation later on.

Birdbrain would always break little rules like that out in the open, leaving him and our platoon vulnerable to attention from high-ranking people we didn't want attention from. As we landed in Kuwait, he was in charge of organizing conexes full of the squadron's gear. A conex is just a big metal container the military uses to transport equipment in. Equipment needed for war! Remember that.

"Sergeant Vance, where's the LT?" Rasp frantically asked.

"No idea. What's up?" I asked.

"The squadron XO (executive officer) wants to know why he isn't present for the arrival of our conexes in the motor pool."

"SHIT!"

"He won't answer the radio either."

Little Birdbrain was off visiting one of his buddies in a completely different unit. Way to go, jackass. Do you know who gets blamed for a butter bar being fucked up? That LT's platoon. The XO had some choice words for him though. While Birdbrain was getting his ass chewed, one of my soldiers approached me with a written letter he found near the LT's cot. It was a love letter to his "fiancé." I really wanted to exploit it, but told the soldier to put it on the LT's nasty cot. Upon his return, Birdbrain was upset with me.

"Sergeant Vance, I don't appreciate people moving my private letters," he said.

"Lieutenant, that letter was found on the ground. A soldier read it to find out whom it belonged to and out of the kindness of *his* heart placed it on *your* cot. If you don't like people touching your stuff, I recommend you tidy up a bit to avoid this situation," I said, verbally cold-cocking him in the face.

"Well I don't think people should be talking about how messy my cot is. You need to tell me if its messed up, sergeant."

"So you want me to tell our highest ranking, highest paid, grown-ass man that graduated from West Point how to keep his area clean so people don't pick on him?"

"If this is a problem I'll go talk to the platoon sergeant."

"Let me know how that works out for ya, lieutenant."

SFC Rasp slapped me on the wrist and asked that I be patient with Birdbrain. I thought I handled it well. Birdbrain just didn't like getting embarrassed by a lowlife enlisted man such as myself. I just glared at my boss like, "really?" And we hadn't even entered a combat zone with this guy.

UGS! And not the Boots with the Fur

"So, what's Uganda like?" I asked the Ugandan guard.

"AIDS," he affirmed with a head nod.

COP Cobra in Diyala Province, near the boarder of Iran, would be our home for the entire deployment as we headed out of Kuwait to Iraq. It was August of 2009 as I explored our miniature base to see how secure the perimeter was.

We were undermanned and running too many missions to also pull guard. In situations like this, we contracted Ugandans, or Ugs. That way we didn't have to worry about asking the corrupt Iraqi army unit stationed with us to pull guard. Insider attacks would have sky rocketed. Ugs are a great bunch to watch your back and do you know why? Of course you don't. It's because they had more disdain for Iraqi's than we did.

Every Ug had very dark complexion, shaved or short hair with minimal facial hair growth and devout Christians. While Iraqi soldiers sported long pinky finger nails to snort cocaine and American soldiers were sneaking off to get high or drink, the Ugs just relaxed around a fire and stayed out of trouble. They dawned tan desert boots, pants, and shirt with a black protective vest and black helmet. They preferred to dress like Americans in movies and not actual soldiers. Soldiers have bloused pants with boots tied and the laces tucked in. The Ugs liked to wear their boots like Americans wear their Timberlands with laces only strewn half way up and the tongue sticking way out with unbloused pants. Thanks a lot Hollywood.

They were always friendly and approachable with us, but damn, if an Iraqi tried to enter COP Cobra without the proper credentials and didn't heed to a search, those Ugs wouldn't hesitate to man handle them. I saw an arrogant Iraqi general refuse to allow the Ugs to search him and they raised their AK-47's in an extremely aggressive posture. The search commenced. They knew their job well and didn't bend the rules for anyone. If they were spooked by anything at night while scanning the fields around the COP, they would just start shooting. There were probably a lot of dead animals in those fields. Perfect mentality for perimeter security and they had the most important thing that the Iraqi's never earned... our trust.

White platoon would be prepping for a mission near the gate and out of curiosity and boredom we'd ask the Ugs to educate us on anything from their culture to why they would do this particular job to learning the language to why the hell they ate so many bananas.

"AIDS?"

"Yes, it's beautiful country, but AIDS everywhere."

"So why would you come to this shit hole?"

"I saving the moneys to go someplace nice innnnn Europe."

"How long are you guys here for?"

"Some stay months. I stay 2 year now. They forget me."

Apparently it was a common occurrence for whoever was in charge of the Ugs to lose track of whose turn it was to go home on vacation. An American in that situation would lose his mind, but these guys kept working since the alternative was to go home to "AIDS" I suppose. Not an ideal situation for any human being. These guys just kept to the rules and did their job day in and day out.

"What's the language you speak?"

"Swahili."

"How would I greet someone in Swahili?"

"Mizooloo. *click*"

"And the proper reply?"

"Mizooloo."

"Again?"

"Yes, it means many things. You can say 'Jambo' too."

"I'm so confused. What's with the clicking noises you guys make when you talk?"

"Some tribes have meaning behind click. My people use it like you use to sigh or laugh or sneer. Not a real word. It's affirmation that shows your level of interest in person or conversation."

"You use big words."

"Mizooloo! *click* Hahaha!"

"You're silly."

God bless the Ugs for protecting us in the most dedicated of ways.

Pull the Pin

"Drill Sergeant, what happens if you fall asleep on watch?" a private asked during basic training in the summer of 2004.

"I'll show you, private. Shut the doors," Drill Sergeant Scarecrow boldly ordered.

DS Scarecrow showed us a video of an independent contractor in Iraq that fell asleep in a bad part of town. He was on Al-Jazeera and masked men slowly severed his head with what seemed to be a dull sword. The image of the man's face going from fighting for his life, to fear of death, to the exact moment he was gone is forever ingrained in my head. It taught me to always have your head on a swivel and watch your own back no matter what.

Now speed up to early 2010 in the village of Tibij, Iraq. We were in the process of handing over control to corrupt ISF (Iraqi Security Forces) with our hands tied behind our backs regarding the rules of engagement and posture while on patrol. We felt like we were soldiers trapped in the position of rent-a-cops.

"If you guys can make it out of this year without losing your mind, you can mentally make it out of anything," I'd constantly tell my guys.

Immense boredom brought the complete opposite of vigilance and offered constant opportunities for the enemy to commit sneak attacks such as infiltrating ISF to hit us hard. ISF were people we had to constantly be around. They of course had weapons and would go on joint patrols with us as the enemy influenced them or they are themselves an infiltrating enemy with nothing but the worst intentions. Threats like this are called "Green on Blue."

With the threat of green on blue always on my mind I tried to keep a comfortable distance from any Iraqi forces while on patrol. On one mission we were to link up with an Iraqi military company and do a dismounted patrol thru Tibij. Tibij was a dustbowl and located near a dead lake that we suspected Al-Qaeda was using as both transportation and a hideout. White Platoon and our Iraqi counterparts were to collect intel from as many people as possible on anything suspicious in the area.

Why was this idea not going to work? This was a shanty town and what few people lived there were most likely threatened by any "new neighbors" that might have strolled by with an arsenal. They weren't going to talk to us, but hey, what else do we have to do? I was given control of a squad of Iraqi's whose leader was nicknamed "Machine Gun." I'm guessing it was because he was carrying a... MACHINE GUN. Some jackass soldier probably called him that and now this dipshit thinks it's an awesome name. You might as well call yourself "stinky bastard with two arms and legs."

Machine Gun had a brown-nosing buddy I'll call Pip. Pip was a scrawny, hyperactive guy who was always in my face trying to tell me things like, "mistah, over here, no good." To which I would reply, "Yes, Pip, blood on the wall, no good. Good job, *guy*." I noticed every time Pip tried to get me to investigate something, Machine Gun was stoically posed on the back of an Iraqi pick-up truck and yes, he still had his machine gun and Rambo style head wrap. Pip had to look back at Machine Gun while flailing his arms in frustration when I refused to go anywhere with him while Machine Gun just stared. This behavior was a red flag to me. Why was Pip so upset and why was he always trying to get Machine Gun's attention?

Later in the patrol I found myself on the outside of a cluster of dirt hut homes while the platoon attempted to make nice with the locals. I was over it so I joined our guys on the outside when Pip frantically came up to me gesturing to follow. I told my guys to stay back and decided to follow Pip to the end of the cluster. I stopped so my soldiers could still have eyes on me only 50 meters away. At that point Pip pointed down a nasty back ally next to Machine Gun's truck. The wind picked up and we already had overcast skies to add to the eerie scene.

Pip changed his innocent demeanor and grabbed my arm. With all my gear on he couldn't succeed in moving me. I noticed his men started to circle and Machine Gun aggressively jumped off his truck to walk towards me. This prompted me to swat Pip's grip from my arm. It all happened so fast.

"Sergeant Vance?!" a soldier yelled from the cluster.

"Hang on!" I hollered.

I needed my guys at a safe distance to possibly light these fuckers up. If White came closer, they would be at risk as well and that would be selfish on my part to invite them into whatever was about to happen. It could have been nothing, but I didn't want any part of an Iraqi home video with shiny swords. This is where my efforts to not get lost in translation went out the window along with my patience. I didn't care if they wanted to show me a super model. I wasn't allowing a sketchy Iraqi to drag me anywhere without my guys and a terp.

As Machine Gun closed in more, Pip jumped at me and violently grabbed my vest to try to get me going in a certain direction. Then I saw the opportunity I was looking for. In moments like this you think, "Just shoot them!" but you have to understand that you don't know the language and it might be a legitimate threat Pip is trying to tell you about. If I shot him, all ISF would then turn on all US military and that's not what I was there for. It still just didn't feel right. In that particular moment I decided to send a message to the Iraqi's to stand down or I'm going to kill everything; even those chickens roaming the streets that won't shut the fuck up, adding to the commotion!

Pip was wearing two black grenades on his vest. As his men drew closer and I was fearful they were going to take me away to be decapitated on Al-Jazeera, I grabbed one of the grenades and slipped my index finger thru the safety pin, pulling on it slightly. Pip's men instantly stopped and his face turned white. I smirked to let him know I was serious.

"No, no, NO! MISTAH NO!" Pip squirmed and squealed.

"Back the FUCK UP. YELLA!" I barked.

You don't have to speak English to understand when an American soldier isn't playing around, but I reinforced it with "Yella," which is Arabic for something along the lines of, "Go away." All the Iraqi's backed up and I slipped the pin back into place. Some of White platoon walked up to see what was going on since the wind masked the yelling. I just told them not to trust these Iraqi's. I smoked a lot of cigarettes that night.

"What was that all about?"

"I think I'm losing my mind."

"Huh?"

"It was nothing. They just needed to be put in check and won't bother us any more."

What Pip didn't know is that I was prepared to give everything in service to my country and to protect my brothers. It could have been nothing, but after what I had seen in over two years of Iraq I wasn't about to trust them in that situation. I had to show a possible enemy that was possibly disguised as a possible friend that we were lunatics, thus making them think twice before messing with an American. They started calling me "Crazy." Everyday after that when we had joint patrols, we all kept our distance as I smiled and shouted "Machine Gun!" as he would hesitantly smile and shout back, "Crazy!" Burn in hell after you rot in Tibij, buddy.

Mythical Bowl of Creatures

CAMEL SPIDERS

"You missed it, man," Courtney said.

"What did I miss?" I asked.

"You know that pregnant camel spider I caught?"

"Yeah?"

"We tossed it in a box and lit it on fire with hand sanitizer."

When we got bored at Cobra, we got creative and perhaps a bit demented... again. Camel spiders were a thing of legend before I actually saw one up close. There were stories and pictures of gigantic creepy crawlies that would get you in your sleep, but they weren't that bad. Don't get me wrong; camel spiders are nasty to deal with, but not to the epic proportions you've probably heard about or seen in seriously obscured photographs.

A typical camel spider is the size of a pack of cigarettes. The ones I encountered didn't crawl like most spiders. They leaped! This is the part that freaked me out. You've got a hand-sized spider 15 feet away and he'll close in on you real fast with quick leaping ability and jumps of 2-3 feet at a time. On top of that, camel spiders weren't poisonous, but they had two pairs of interlocking fangs that would tear into anything they grabbed onto, making for an unpleasant encounter. They also made a hissing noise that sounded like a cat's, but since they are much smaller than a cat, it came off as a whispering mini hiss. True story.

Courtney came up with an idea to trap one without getting torn up. He took a concertina wire glove and tossed it within striking distance of the camel spider. Being territorially threatened, the spider leaped and latched on with his four fangs. The C-wire glove is made to protect the hand from sharp objects, so once the spider bit into the glove, Courtney had just enough time to shove him into an empty Gatorade bottle before it could get loose. A stroke of genius.

That bottle may or may not have been an empty piss bottle, making the spider *really* angry. Courtney hit the jackpot as this was no ordinary camel spider. It was a pregnant one and a lot more robust than the others we had caught. We must destroy this beast before it gives birth to more vermin! How? Burn it at the stake! The crowd watching was probably much like the crowds during the Salem Witch Trials screaming, "It's the devil!" Don't sit there reading this and judge our actions on boredom.

SCORPIONS

"There's like, these things coming from under the ground," Gonzo said.

What Gonzo was referring to were scorpions. It was late at night when the rains came. White platoon had two soldiers manning an OP, or observation post. We were responsible for that OP a few days at a time to over-watch a checkpoint that was blinded by the trenched hills where the Iraq/Iran war raged during the 1980's in eastern Diyala Province. It was a dry place, but with a pathetic river running thru it, there was room for life. Albeit not the kind of life you want to see in the middle of the night.

The rain would bring scorpions to the surface in droves. Our guys had to do what they could to stay off the ground. We just lit the area with chem lights to keep an eye on things. There wasn't a lot we could do for scorpion bites with minimal scorpion kits back at Cobra. A funny thing about scorpions is that it's the small whitish-pinkish-translucent... ish looking ones you have to worry about instead of the big-ass black ones. The black ones can still kill, but the little guys kill faster with a higher dose. So how can bored soldiers turn this into a good time? Trap one and toss it in the burn box with a camel spider to see which one wins. It's only natural, right? The scorpion wins every time with a venomous strike from the tail as the spider focuses its attack on the scorpion's front claws. Fatal mistake. Then we burn both of them. "It's the devil!"

PACK THE BOWL

"Whatchya got there?" I asked Wai-Tai.

"I saw that lizard crawling on the T-wall and threw a rock at it," he replied.

"One shot, one kill!" White Toast proclaimed.

"Hell yeah," I added.

"After it fell I tossed it into the 'Mythical Bowl of Creatures' over there."

Wai-Tai put a bowl next to our sad campfire on Cobra and as critters popped up, we hunted them and added them to the bowl. We found foot long lizards, scorpions, camel spiders, hedgehogs and field mice. At the checkpoint we found even more. We took on wild dogs as our pets, watched foxes circle our perimeter and birds half the size of a human torso nosedive to catch rodents. We fancied them the "Birds of Pandora" since they carried such strong colors of red or green and looked like they would be one of James Cameron's creations from Avatar.

At night we turned on huge lights to keep the perimeter well lit at the checkpoint. This is where the action was. I had never seen so many insects in such a small area. It rivaled the house raids we did in Baghdad during my first deployment where we entered a house and the floor appeared to move because there were so many flies. Insects rose from the river towards the lights and it resembled a snowstorm with zero visibility, only it was 120 degrees. Bats, smaller birds and bigger insects would swoop in all night until their stomachs could hold no more. Darwinism at its finest.

Tippin Cox

White was on QRF when we got a call to come pick some people up at the TOC and give them a ride in a Stryker around COP Cobra like a fucking kid on a pony at a county fair. I had no idea that the Marlboro-looking gentleman standing out of the hatch next to me was none other than country star, Aaron Tippin. I thought we were giving some politician a ride for what we call a "Dog and Pony Show" where we pretend to be happy and get cleaned up for high-ranking personnel. Not the case this time. Tippin was quiet and completely respectful while on our Stryker. We took him for a lap and dropped him off so he could play a few songs for the rest of the COP.

Tippin stopped by with a small entourage and Fox news contributor Bill Cox. Cox had some hilarious stories from his time in Vietnam, but out of complete respect for him I'll keep those between him and us. I had to leave their appearance early for QRF purposes, but I heard Tippin played five songs and had to leave. I asked Mikey to ask both men to sign my guitar and they did so without hesitation. That guitar hangs high in my house today.

Its not a celebrities job to "support the troops" or not cry over a broken nail and report it on twitter, but it means so much to people overseas to simply make an appearance. Just think of all the emotional times, whether good or bad, like at a wedding or a funeral in your life. Now think about how good it felt to see someone's face as they walked thru the door to hug you during those emotional times. You didn't care what they had to give you or what they had to say. You only cared that they were there. That's how people overseas feel when celebrities simply show up and we'll always be thankful.

Kick the Puppies

On my first deployment we would do some reconnaissance on a house where a target lived. If a neighborhood dog came out to bark, then the target would know Americans were close by. The reason for this is because Iraqi's would beat the hell out of dogs and the dogs would therefore never bark at a local out of fear. This led us to believe we had to instill fear in the canines as well. When doing our recon of a house to raid, I would shoot any barking dog with our non-lethal paintball gun right between the eyes. The dog would then associate our smell and sound with pain, thus instilling a fear that kept them quiet when we snuck in at night. It was comical to see a dog come running out to investigate, then slowly back up and hide without making a peep. My second deployment was very different. Dogs just seemed to get in the way. They liked us so much it literally killed them.

"Ok, I tried yelling and throwing rocks at it to scare the little bastard away, but it's still sitting there shaking between the right 2 and 3 tires," I said.

"Is he close enough to grab?" Whitey asked.

"Not with all this gear on."

"We don't have time to crawl under there either."

"White Toast, just creep us out to start off and maybe it'll run away when the tires slowly start to roll."

"Roger that," said White Toast and we started to move...

"*YIP!*" went the last sound that little white fluff ball of a dog would ever make as we flattened it to death.

"Ohhhhh shit!" went the entire truck.

"I fuckin' warned 'em," I pleaded for an excuse to make this right.

We all got quiet after that. There we were, a bunch of roughnecks at each other's throats everyday and we felt bad about a third world dog too confused to move.

"Puppy down," I declared as its remnants disappeared in the dust.

I know what you're thinking. Members of White platoon went around kicking puppies. We may joke about it, but that's not the case. We weren't the guys you see on the Internet tossing puppies off of cliffs or drowning them in rivers. We liked dogs. Sometimes we just had no choice. We treated Iraqi dogs like royalty compared to Iraqis themselves. Dogs are seen as gross animals and constantly treated like shit by locals. Dogs flocked to us when we were living at a checkpoint with Iraqis and Kurds. We could provide food and affection. This is something the locals never gave. I have a feeling the dogs felt safer around us as well, but were they?

"Sergeant Vance you might wanna come up here and take a look at this mess!" Hall yelled from the high ground at the checkpoint where our Stryker was about to park.

"Roger," I said, hoping it wasn't something ridiculous the previous platoon had left behind.

As I got to Hall's position I saw him just looking at the ground. My eyes moved to where his were looking and didn't know what to think about what I saw as my eyebrows went way up.

"How the hell did this happen?" I asked.

"Fuckin' Crapp backed his driver up right over it," Hall replied.

"And they just took off?"

"Yup! I'll get a bag and shovel.

"That's sad... and disgusting."

What Hall was looking at was a dead dog with four blue look-ing puppies strewn up to eight feet from its belly. Crapp backed his Stryker up over a pregnant dog and out popped four unborn puppies. All dead. Not a pretty sight, BUT an accident. Damn dogs thinking they should hide by some tires. There's some kind of magnetizing ef-fect tires have on dogs and it gets them killed too often. At least we still had Roxy, our checkpoint dog. We looked after her better than we looked after ourselves after the blue puppy incident.

Places to Poo

PROPER POO DISPOSAL

"Sergeant Stache! Are we supposed to piss in these too?" I hollered from a nearby culvert.

"Uh, no I don't think so!" SGT Stache yelled back.

"Damn it."

While working with boarder patrol agents on the Mexican boarder in October and November of 2005 we had to be very careful to hide our existence. A measure I believed to be most unnecessary in that instance. Each Stryker was given one plastic 5-gallon bucket to bring to their position on the boarder. These crafty little midg-a-Johns came with plastic bags and a seat. The trick was that we were only allowed to poo in these plastic bags. I don't know about you, but if I go number 2, it's usually followed by going number 1. So essentially we had to poo while slinging our wangs over the side of the bucket. This would be the most awkward poo I would ever make. I wondered how a woman could do this successfully. Every day our First Sergeant and his driver would stop by and pick up the bags-o-poo. He and his driver then went to a disposal area, opened each bag and then dumped the remnants. They had to do all that for the environment and to hide our existence. An environment that nobody inhabited, except for the boarder jumpers passing thru. Makes a lot of sense doesn't it? The smell of opening those bags had to be quite lovely. That's what I call paying your dues and hats off to the First Sergeant and his driver.

THIS IS HAPPENING

"Vance, you OK?" Lebel asked.

"Yeah, it's that time," I replied with a pale face.

"Time for what?"

"Time to piss out of my ass."

"You just ate ten minutes ago."

"Yep, then I'm late.

I scurried out of the chow hall in Taji, Iraq in the spring of 2010 hoping to make it to the latrine on the other side of the compound. No such luck.

"Shit, shit, shit oh no, this isn't happening," I whimpered to myself.

Oh but it is, Mat, **IT IS**. There was no way I could make it to the other side of the compound for an actual toilet, but I scanned the area for a shack with "hodgy shitters" where I could do the whole "squat to poo in a hole in the ground" thing. I spotted a shack and awkwardly ran in as I clinched my ass cheeks while still whimpering.

"No, no, no you don't."

I dropped my pants around my ankles while I was still a few feet away from the hole, spun my body around to get into position, grabbed a wall and down I went in a sweaty heap thinking I was about to expel Lucifer himself right out of my bunghole.

"Ohhhhh yeah," I moaned in both relief and pain.

That'll teach me to eat local food that's prepared with unfiltered river water. My average sized body had dysentery for a few weeks and dropped 20 pounds thanks to completely liquidating all consumed food in about ten minutes. From the moment food went down my throat, it waged a violent war with my digestive track letting out screams from within to let me know that I had better find a place for the casualties real quick. There were no solid pieces either. It was all acidy liquid that burned all the chafed skin from where I would wipe at least nine times in 24 hours. Dehydration is a motherfucker. To this day, I only purchase premium Charmin's.

Going number two is taken for granted every day back in the States. Did you know it's actually better for your digestive track to squat over a hole in the ground and the way you're used to sitting on the toilet actually creates hemorrhoids? Squatters apparently know a thing or two about poo. Squatting is the hard part, but by no means the nasty part. Luckily on that day in Taji, I had already been dealing with the issue since I was in Diyala Province two weeks earlier. That means I knew I had to carry an emergency supply of toilet paper at all times. If I hadn't had the TP with me in the shack, I would have had to go "third world" on the wiping. That would entail hoping there was still water in the hose lying next to the hole to rinse while wiping with my hand. That's why Iraqi's don't shake with their left hand and to offer yours is extremely insulting.

QUESTIONABLE EVOLUTION

I've stayed in some really nice places while deployed, but then again I've also stayed in places where even rats are like, "Oh, hell no." At COP Cobra, we had to improvise when it came to our bowel needs. There were nice porcelain holes in the ground, but it's not easy to squat and aim with all of our gear on. We first grabbed a metallic folding chair and cut out an ass-sized hole in the seat. Duck tape was put over the sharp metal from our primitive cutting job and we then placed the chair over the porcelain hole in the ground. Great success! However, the local plumbing still couldn't handle TP. After wiping, we had to put the used TP in a trash bag sitting next to the makeshift toilet. Yes, that meant if some mouth-breathing degenerate decided to miss the trash we all got a whiff and a few lucky ones got an accidental touch of someone else's feces all over their hand.

Eventually engineers made it out to Cobra and installed toilets. All good, right? Negative. We shared those latrines with the Iraqi military. They couldn't get a handle on "sitting." Instead of sitting on the toilet to do their business, they would stand on top of the toilet seat and squat. As you can imagine, they missed. The toilet seat would look like somebody dropped mud on it and then leaped all over to the sounds of "Kris Kross will make you jump, jump!"

BURN IT

"If I was going to be a shit burner, I made damn sure I was the best shit burner we'd ever had," Coach Lyons ranted.

Coach Lyons was referring to his service back in Vietnam. At the time of this speech, I was riding the bench as usual attempting to play college football at Christopher Newport University. I never complained about being on the bench because I knew college was the wrong time to start playing. I was in it purely to try something new and man, I was the worst player on that team. However, a lot of other bench-ridden players were crying about the splinter collection in their asses from riding the pine.

Good ole Coach Lyons decided to do a motivational speech to teach them how to be team players. He explained that everyone has a place and if people don't take their jobs seriously, the whole team falls apart. Coach Lyons explained that back in Vietnam, as an FNG, he was told to burn shit. Instead of complaining about the nasty job, he did it the best he could until he was promoted. A lot of guys on the team might have forgotten that speech, but it served me well as a leader. Thank you, sir.

I was lucky enough to never have been told to burn shit due to my position or rank, but I didn't think that was right. During my second tour I always included myself in the shit burning rotation. It can be pretty demoralizing to burn somebody's excrement that doesn't share the same duties, no pun intended, so I think it would behoove every leader to join in the fun.

So how do you burn shit? Very easy and the smell is unforgettable! Grab a 10 gallon metal bucket for everyone to shit in. All full? Drag that fucker out in the open away from anything flammable or edible. It's recommended to dump just a cup of diesel fuel in the shit bucket, but I'm a pyromaniac so I encouraged the guys to do a "healthy pour." Light a MRE match and drop it in. Man-make-fire! Man-make stinky fire. Start stirring. Depending on the load, everything should be evaporated after 30-45 minutes of stirring with a 4-5 foot metal pole. Add more diesel as necessary. Now you're a big boy. Go brag about this war story at the bar and let me know how many digits you land.

MOST CREATIVE DROP

While deployed, our schedule could go from insane to complete boredom on the daily. Along with an extremely new environment, new diet, adjusting to vaccines and of course sleep depravation, our bowel cycle was all kinds of FUBAR. When Mother Nature called, you had no choice but to answer. Often times we weren't in a natural place to make it happen, so we had to improvise.

If we were on a dismounted patrol that came to a halt, guys would just walk a few feet off the path or road to drop a deuce. If we were clearing a house, guys would leave a present for whoever dwelled there to come home to and it wasn't in a toilet. Sick, I know, but we giggled like little girls after leaving homes with such "presents." The most difficult time to poo was when we were in a moving Stryker. Some guys would just open the back hatch located on the ramp, squat with their bare asses hanging out of the back of the Stryker and drop a turd. From the side it definitely looked like the Stryker itself was shitting all over the street, much like a horse without care.

Zach Brown, not the country star, takes the cake with the most creative attempt. Notice the word "attempt." I met Zach after my first tour and he's become one of my best friends. There's never a dull moment in his life. Zach went thru a world of shit before the military, yet I've only known him to be an outstanding person and soldier. He's tall, white, had peppered hair before his 23rd birthday, loves all things Baltimore and can party like Yancey. One thing about Zach is that he wasn't afraid to put aside his pride to make others laugh. This mentality allowed him to do whatever he wanted in front of other people with no shame.

So no shit there he was (I have to stop with these puns). Zach was inside a Stryker on the move. He was riding in a mortar variant. The mortar variant had an actual mortar tube on the inside and the roof of the Stryker would open like a French door to allow the mortar tube to fire at a moments notice. Zach's vehicle could essentially drop a bomb (I did that pun on purpose) down the tube and it would then fly out of the Stryker en route to killing the enemy. Zach however would use this tube for a different kind of mission.

Zach really had to go number 2, but his platoon couldn't safely stop. He grabbed a plastic bag, threw it in the mortar tube as if it were a makeshift trashcan and tried to hop on. There was a problem with the angle of the tube and the bumpy road his platoon was traveling on. Zach literally had to jump multiple times while grabbing at whatever he could to balance himself to attempt this feat. He not only got some in the bag successfully, but he got it everywhere else as well. That included the floor, equipment and possibly dudes. Probably not a good experience for the rest of the mortar platoon inside that Stryker, but I love laughing while thinking of that story.

Food

YOU FIRST

We had a meeting with a chicken farmer who was wealthy by local standards. Our retarded fucking lieutenant thought that because this chicken fucker, I mean farmer, was rich he would talk to us about "terrorists." Birdbrain never understood the difference between a terrorist, an insurgent and local militia. We sat on the floor in the farmer's "living room" and he gestured at us to eat the breakfast that was laid out on the dirt-covered floor.

"He want you to eat food," our terp informed us.

"I'm good, man," I said.

"But now you're rude. You must eat."

"You know what's rude? Dysentery. I will not eat this shit."

Spread out on the floor was sour cream and a sad attempt at over easy eggs. The sour cream looked more like sausage gravy. The eggs were way undercooked and a bit on the watery side. To wash all that down we could have chi, or tea, with more sugar than chi or warm river water with random floaters... mmmmmm... NEGATIVE.

"Sergeant Vance, we shouldn't be rude," Birdbrain said.

"Oh, well then you won't mind going first, LT," I glared back.

Birdbrain had one bite and it was all over. Not so rude now, is it? If the local food doesn't look right, it's a safe bet not to eat it. Common sense goes a long ways. It goes a lot longer than "not being rude." That's just how Birdbrain was wired. Any local could invite him into their house and he'd go right in without any backup. Never mind that it might have a torture chamber, machetes and a video camera broadcasting his beheading worldwide on Al-Jazeera. We argued many times over how to do things safely and after he had enough of me advising him on how foolish he was and proceeded to ignore me, people got hurt. In situations like eating bad food, I enjoyed telling Birdbrain to do what ever the hell he wanted because he got burned every time.

MRE CHALLENGE

"Alright Mitch, how many MRE's can you take down in a 24 hour period?" I asked.

"A whole case," he replied.

"Bullshit."

"Aight, game on."

An MRE, or Meal Ready to Eat, is a specially packaged meal that will last a long, long time while still in the plastic. That alone should raise some eyebrows. It was great if you were starving or just bored out of your mind trying to stay awake during mission. We typically rat-fucked them. No, that's not a sexual reference. That term just means that we opened an MRE and took the food we wanted or needed for a certain time frame, much like a rat takes what it wants and scurries off.

MRE's weren't only used to quench our hunger. Certain things inside those packages were remedies for issues you may have during missions with little medical supplies available. For instance, if you were pissing out of your ass and desperately needed something to back up your bowels so you didn't wipe yourself to death, you would grab the cheese packets. The cheese in an MRE could back you up for days at a time or at least until you had stomach pain from being backed up. At that point you would grab the gum packet or dry chocolate shake. All you had to do was add the right amount of water to the shake and *POW*, instant ex lax.

Mitch took the MRE challenge and if anyone could eat 12 MRE's in a single day without crapping, it would be him. He was a legit body builder always aiming to be 270 pounds of brute force and become the next Mr. Olympia. In order to gain copious amounts of weight he would need to eat a lot of calories to keep up with his workout regimen. A case of MRE's designed to give maximum calories would be great, right? The problem with eating 12 MRE's from the same case is the lack of food selection. Mitch had to eat everything in every meal. That included the always-dreaded "Southwest Breakfast Omelet." A stench filled the area as soon as the packet was opened and it looked like regurgitated Play-Doe with green and red chunks placed sporadically that were allegedly "peppers." Good luck, buddy!

"Times up. How many?

"Eleven."

"So close!"

"Yo, I just couldn't do it, man."

"How's the stomach?"

"I need to get to a toilet."

KITCHEN RAID

Although we were working out of a COP, we still encountered a lot of characters that weren't in combat arms. We didn't always mesh well with these types. Of course they are nice to have around when you need someone with a specialized job. Night vision techs would fix our NODS while listening to heavy metal or screamo for hours on end while inside a small conex. Mechanics worked their asses off fixing our Strykers in extreme heat and would roll out with us to fix something, putting their lives on the line. Then there were the cooks. Is it nice to have cooks? Yes. Is completely great to have cooks? No.

The cooks at COP Cobra asked that we send soldiers to help them out between our missions. We did so even though our guys didn't have much time off in the first place. After listening to some of my soldiers gripe about how the cooks are making them do all the work, which included heavy lifting and cleaning some nasty equipment, we investigated. Sure as shit, there were our soldiers doing all the work while the higher-ranking cooks were sitting back, getting fat. That ended our 'Helping of the Crooks' mission. Then they retaliated.

On certain days, the cooks would claim they were being over worked and set out MRE's or Jimmy Dean's packages. After being on a mission that lasted several days and coming back to more crap-tastic chow, we gave them the coup de grau.

"Time for a raid gentlemen," I suggested.

"Sergeant Vance, I know where they keep all the good shit," Perma-Fried said.

"Like what?"

"Like those Gatorade shakes that they've been stingy with," Courtney added.

My guys made nice with lower-ranking cooks and gathered the majority of the shakes. They brought them back to our platoon living area to share. We filled our bellies with ice-cold chocolate milk shakes in a can courtesy of Gatorade that night. Liquid gold! That coupled with cigarettes and shit-eating grins was enough to make us think we just had a good day. Small things like that allowed us to make it another day without going crazy.

The cooks were furious, but never found out who owned them that night. Each time we came back to Cobra and there was a convenient food shortage, we raided those bastards and took anything we could while they slept.

There was another option on certain days of the week. If the cooks closed shop we went to the hodgy stand. This guy didn't have a TV with hot Americans like the first deployment, but his food was A.M.A.Z.I.N.G. Say what you want about my claim, but pizza is the single most important invention and this man brought us a little taste of home with his creative Iraqi pizza stand. Fresh fruit, fresh chicken, oven roasted pita bread and if you're not in the mood for pizza, which is a travesty in itself, then go with the gyro, which I controversially pronounced 'euro.' Bon appétit.

SNORT THIS

Sometimes we would resort back to the basic training boredom killer of ingesting things we shouldn't for a little extra cash. Justin Courtney took one for the team one night. Courtney was about 5'8," brown haired and held immense strength for someone his size, so we dubbed him "Mighty Mouse." Prior to working out most of the guys would take supplements. One such supplement was called Jack3D. It came in a white powder form and resembled cocaine. Well, White platoon was bored and wanted to see somebody snort a line of Jack3D just to see what happened. Courtney took this opportunity, rolled up a dollar bill and lined up the product with a CAC card.

Sniiiiiiiiiiiiiiff

"Awww it BURNS!" Courtney grimaced.

"Ohhhhh!" went the platoon.

What did Courtney get for this? Six bucks. He was bouncing off the walls all night and I'm pretty sure he didn't sleep for a couple of days. Was this a healthy and wise decision? Not even close, but it gave White platoon yet another escape as Courtney looked all tweaked out for a while. He wouldn't be the only guy to snort something inappropriate that tour.

Charles Olson decided that he was going to snort a line of snuff. Snuff is a granular form of tobacco. It's one thing to sniff a little at a time, but Olson was going to do an entire line. Olson was tall with a husky build, dark brown hair and quiet. He's very intelligent and when he spoke up, everyone, especially myself, listened intently. Our previous LT, Jamal, nicknamed him MC, or Monster Cock. Apparently Jamal walked in on a naked MC changing one day and decided to just throw in a nickname to laugh at the situation. MC chopped the snuff more finely than it already was on a Stryker Ramp.

Sniiiiiiiiiiiiff

"Yep, it burns," MC calmly stated.

MC wasn't kept awake for days, but he provided more entertainment and an escape for a bunch of guys at his own expense. Whether it was drugs, alcohol, snorting workout powder or tobacco products we found creative ways to stay sane. What would you do if you were away from your home and family for a year in a war zone? You just stopped judging us didn't you?

Burn Toppy Burn: Part Deux

Oh boy, what's next with this guy? How about a story surrounding a stuffed animal and soft-core porn? After we headed north into Iraq, we discovered something odd about Birdbrain. He had a Beanie Baby sized giraffe he named Toppy. Toppy would go everywhere with Birdbrain. The reason for this is because his alleged fiancé gave it to him and he wanted to take pictures with high-ranking Iraqi officials and send them to her. Well, as you can imagine, Birdbrain got sloppy.

The first problem was that he wasn't very sneaky in the placement of Toppy. He would walk into meetings with the damn thing sticking out of his cargo pocket for everyone to gawk at in strange curiosity. Birdbrain would then walk out to the trucks after a meeting, grinning. His grin was so awkward. Our medic, Meany (that's his real name, because he's awesome) dubbed him "Double Chops" since he would clinch his teeth and open his lips as far as possible, completely exposing both rows of teeth. It was cartoonish in nature. Both his smile and an exposed Toppy were not helping Birdbrain's position with the platoon. The second problem he had was disclosing too much information to a platoon that despised him. He would always bitch to us about issues with his fiancé.

"Well, we're from Vegas and she's going to live there while I'm deployed, but I don't know why she still has to share a storage unit with her ex-fiancé," he questioned.

Maybe because she's sleeping with him! I couldn't say that though.

"Yeah that's so weird," I'd say with a blank stare and innocent smile.

The dumbass even got sloppy with the placement of his girl doing an awful striptease, much like Jamie Lee Curtis' performance for Arnold in "True Lies." One night at the checkpoint it was my turn to sleep, so off I went into the hellhole of the Stryker. Mitch, who was on watch at the time, awakened me. He didn't say anything, because he didn't want to wake up the LT, who was sleeping only a few feet away. Mitch just gave me the universal symbol for "keep quiet" with his index finger over his lips and showed me a video on his cell phone. It was some woman doing a terrible dance in lingerie.

"I don't get it, man," I whispered.

"That's the LT's chick!" he whispered back as he tried not the laugh.

"How?"

"I asked if I could get some music from his phone to listen to and he gave it up. I uploaded *EVERYTHING!*"

That video made its way around the entire platoon and he never knew. Score one for the good guys. Of course we all made references to chicks making videos for us, but he never picked up on it. Shocking.

The last screw up with Toppy and its connection to his fiancé was not securing Toppy after he pissed us off to the point where we had to take action. In Vietnam, LT's like Birdbrain would "disappear," but we couldn't do that and get away with it so we had to get creative. We had to attack something close to his heart. One day he left Toppy unsecured on the truck. With my crew, that was a mistake. Especially after he recently made the platoon give back peanut butter Cliff Bars we "acquired" fair and square from those damn cooks at Cobra. Those were like gold when meals were sparse.

We decided to kidnap Toppy and hold him hostage. We offered his freedom for our Cliff Bars in a ransom note written in Arabic by one of our terps along with a picture of me and Mikey fully masked like "terrorists" holding a grenade next to Toppy's head. Birdbrain was such a dumb prick that he only offered straight up cups of peanut butter after translating the letter and claiming he could figure out who was in the picture. He never found out who was in the picture or that the terp that translated the letter for him was in on the joke with the terp that wrote it.

When we refused to release Toppy he threatened to talk to higher. Wow, he wants to tell the commander that somebody has his precious stuffed animal? The commander would have reamed Birdbrain, but then we would hear about it and we didn't want that kind of attention. What a douche. We released the giraffe... temporarily.

JD, Mikey and myself were bitching about how poorly a mission went one day and decided to take it out on the innocent giraffe.

"I'd burn that motherfucker right now if I had 'em," Mikey stated.

"You would?" JD asked in a tone I hadn't heard him use before. "Birdbrain is in a meeting right now and I know exactly where Toppy is."

"Lets do this," I instigated.

JD grabbed Toppy from Birdbrain's sleeping area and handed it to Mikey. Mikey stuffed it in a box we had gotten in the mail and we lit the fire. Toppy went up in smoke as platoon members came out to be by the fire. The three of us had to keep it a secret until everything blew over.

For the rest of the tour we played dumb when Birdbrain asked about Toppy. He threatened to do an inspection of everything we had to find it. We said no. It was a glorious victory watching him squirm at the loss of the only thing left that connected him to his unfaithful fiancé. Oh, but the fun isn't over yet, folks...

LT's were responsible for accountability reports on all equipment in the platoon. Birdbrain was actually signed for an expensive Leopold scope that came up missing. One of our soldiers said they had seen the LT take the scope out of its storage bag and place it on top of our Stryker during a mission. Birdbrain denied this. He made us dump everything out of all the trucks after a mission in the middle of an Iraqi summer. We had to lay everything out in a fancy, organized fashion. Then we told his highness everything was ready to be searched. He found nothing. Birdbrain then searched our personal items... twice. He found nothing. The process from our mission that morning to the end of his inspections went from sun up to damn near midnight. Everyone wanted to curb-stomp his face.

One day while out on patrol we stopped by an Iraqi military post in Tibij. Out of a field an Iraqi soldier came walking up with a pipe-shaped object while pointing at Birdfuck. Oh hell no. It was the scope worth thousands of dollars that had been missing. That turd lied about not taking it out and putting it on top of the Stryker. Birdbrain left it on the Stryker during a night mission and it flew off after we hit a few bumps. He just laughed with joy, because now he didn't have to pay for it. We loathed him as no apology was given.

Soldiers in White started to openly show their disgust after that. Birdbrain got testy with one in particular. Specialist Rogers was our Military Intelligence soldier that collected and analyzed all the intel we were getting. He also interrogated people for information. Rogers was an asset to White and unfortunately he had to work as closely with the LT as I did. Since nobody was giving respect to Birdbrain, he tried to force it on the lower-ranking soldiers, such as Rogers.

"Sergeant Vance, I want Rogers to address me as sir," Birdbrain announced.

"Excuse me?" I snapped.

"I don't like how he calls me LT."

"Well...*LT*, Rogers is authorized to call you sir, LT or lieutenant."

I had no idea if that was true, but he was so scared of me it worked. For you young leaders out there, you need to earn that salute or title through gaining the respect of your subordinates. You *never* ask for it, because if you do, then you've lost it forever. I was an enlisted soldier and people saluted me at times in approval for something I did. It was a joke, but still a sign of approval. I introduced myself as Vance, not Sergeant Vance, but people still called me Sergeant. Not everyone is going to respect you or like you, but don't ever ask to be called something you haven't earned.

You've got to be wondering how this guy reacts in combat! We received a call from an Iraqi military unit in Asadiyah about an IED on the road. It wasn't our platoon's AO, but we were on QRF that day and escorted EOD to the site. Was that enough abbreviations for you? We rolled up and stopped a few hundred meters away from the IED on the road.

"I want to dismount and check this out," Birdbrain said.

"That's not a good idea since this isn't our AO. For all we know, we're parked in the same spot third platoon parks in when they get a call about an IED in that same spot," I advised.

"So?"

"So that could be a decoy IED and the real one is waiting for us to jump off these Strykers."

"I want to over-watch EOD."

"At least keep everyone else on the trucks to minimize targets on the ground. We haven't cleared any of these buildings or that cemetery on the other side of the street."

"White 4, White 1, I'm dismounting with White 1 Tango and the terp. Everyone else stay on the trucks."

"This is White 4, Roger," JD said back.

The air was filled with dust and visibility was down to just under a mile. Something bad always seemed to happen under those conditions. We started our walk and I noticed White 3 took a couple of soldiers into a nearby courtyard to help clear the area against Birdbrain's instructions. He claimed not hearing those instructions and Lt apparently didn't hear White 3 say he was dismounting. This is why communication is key and saves lives.

BOOM!

I felt the concussion of the blast push thru my body as my bones shuttered and debris flew all over as I managed to stay on my feet. My ears were ringing as my other senses heightened. AK-47 gunfire rang out as the Iraqi soldiers commenced with what they do best, the death blossom, which is spraying bullets aimlessly in all directions in fear. I turned to check for casualties and actually had a split second of comedic relief.

"LT! Terp!" I yelled.

The terp was just in a slight daze, but Birdbrain was literally crouched down and spinning in circles with his head down almost like that game where you spin around ten times with your forehead on the handle of a baseball bat that's touching the ground. It was hilarious! Everyone reacts differently to contact, but that was by far the funniest. I grabbed both men and directed them to cover and climbed up the side of one of the Strykers to talk to the gunner.

"Hey! 3 Golf! Where's White 3's team!" I screamed fearing the worst.

"I think the courtyard!" he hollered while pointing.

You think? Right. I climbed back down and told Birdbrain and the terp to stay behind me so we can check on White 3 and his team.

"4, 1 Tango, I'm going into the courtyard to check for casualties," I said on the net.

"This is 4, roger," JD said back with a quickness.

A little bit of panic set in, because some of the guys on White 3's team were mine and he told me he was taking them for the mission. I didn't approve, but I didn't have a choice since he outranked me. Thanks to White 3 not hearing the radio calls to stay on the truck and Birdbrain not heeding to my warnings, lives were in danger. As we ran into the courtyard the three soldiers were holding each other up and moving to the exit. The blast had thrown all three into a wall of the building inside the courtyard. My team secured their movement as we went back to the trucks to assess casualties.

"Hall! Drop the ramp!" I yelled to the back hatch plug.

Something was wrong with Hall. He could see me yelling, but he couldn't understand me. Hall saw the wounded soldiers moving towards him and dropped the ramp.

"You OK Hall?" I asked.

"I can't hear shit!" he yelled.

The blast was right next to his Stryker and his head was completely exposed at half the distance I was. The blast in the courtyard was the back blast area and not as strong, but it still managed to throw three men over 200 lbs into a wall. The main force of the blast hit Hall on the other side of the courtyard wall in the street and then ten feet later hit my team. It blew his eardrum out and gave him a nasty concussion.

White headed back to Cobra for medical attention. The gate was blocked by local construction crews trying to get on the compound, so Swanny jumped on top of his Stryker while he was gunning and took matters into his own hands in the name of helping his brothers. This made for an intimidating spectacle towards the locals as it looked like Swanny was surfing a moving Stryker while screaming savagely.

"Hey! Get the *FUCK* out of the way! Fucking *MOVE!*" he screamed.

The locals didn't have to speak the same language to understand that if they didn't move, they were going to be the next casualties via Swanny's wrath. Well played, Swanny. We dropped our walking wounded off at the squadron medical trailer and returned to the gate to park until we were called out again.

"1 Tango, this is White 4," JD said to me over the net.

"This is 1 Tango," I replied.

"Yeah, you gotta come up here and get evaluated for a concussion."

I could tell it wasn't his choice so I complied even though we both knew I've had worse blows to the noggin. As I arrived, I couldn't help but notice our little LT was feeling sorry for himself and that day was his first brush with death. Aw, need a hug little guy? JD had a funny conversation with our troop commander.

"Sergeant, why is your LT trying to get a purple heart for a concussion?"

The entire platoon bellowed in laughter when we caught wind of this conversation. What a pussy. That's why he had me called me up to the medics. He knew if I requested it, people would listen. Well, I don't believe in requesting a Purple Heart for myself, especially when there was no loss of blood. He was shit out of luck. Traumatic brain injuries are a whole other discussion. Score another one for the good guys. Birdbrain was also one of those guys that received a Combat Action Badge for a mortar round that landed on the opposite side of a compound, nowhere close to being a threat to him.

Birdbrain represented everything a soldier shouldn't be. He wanted awards and respect without earning them. I saw a growing number of soldiers like this as my time in the service came to an end. What can you do? I say raise awareness of dirt bags by making fun of them mercilessly in the form of reading material. We must teach future generations of the intangibles required to be good leaders.

Otherwise... stay the fuck out of the United States Military. 'Merica.

The military had lost too much of its gusto for me to stay. It was finally time to go home and feel normal again. I couldn't go on arguing with the likes of Birdbrain as too many good guys were getting hurt and the turds were getting promoted.

NORMALCY?

I made the decision to get out of the military during that last deployment. I knew I would miss the camaraderie and action, but the bullshit in between was too much. There were 42-year-old soldiers that looked 70. That's not what I wanted for my future. What would it be like to become a civilian again? Would I become lazy? Would people understand me? Should I get a helmet so oranges don't give me concussions? What is normal?

Me Bum Bum!

"You drop your pants and put hands on table," ordered the doctor.

"Huh?" I questioned.

"Final part of exam... prostate check."

"I mean, I didn't ask for that and didn't know about it until now."

"It's part of exam. We have to."

I was back in the States and ready to be a civilian again. Getting out of the military was a hilarious process. Everyone out-processing has to get a physical so the VA can ASSess your health. I was under the impression it would be a quick check up since the physicals we got while in the service were... nonexistent, but it turned into a day of uncomfortable probing. The physician who gave me the exam looked like Mr. Chow from the Hangover movies and spoke just like him too. So now I have an aggressive little man ordering me to drop my pants.

I walked into a private room and dropped trou next to one of those elevated pleather seats with loud, white paper on top of it. A very attractive female nurse walked in and stood next to the counter top with a clipboard. All right, maybe this won't be as bad as I thought and we'll have some fun with it. Then Mr. Chow walked in with his aggressive posture and strapped on latex gloves. He then moved towards me with a tiny tube of lube. My rear end clinched as my eyes widened. I guess the attractive nurse won't be doing this task and I won't be having a "Road Trip" moment. Or would I?

I turned to hold onto the pleather seat and Mr. Chow went for it. The process was awkward and physically uncomfortable. He used a whole lot of lube and I definitely held a yuck face of disapproval the entire time. When Mr. Chow was done checking everything, I was expecting words of comfort or something like, "Everything checked out fine," but that wasn't the case.

The cute nurse turned to walk out with a slight smile on her face. I bet she enjoyed the show. As for Mr. Chow, he tossed his gloves in the trash and washed his hands. My pants are still down, mind you, and I'm feeling a bit vulnerable. He then grabbed a box of Kleenex's and turned to me with his judging eyes. Mr. Chow then tossed the box at my chest. I didn't even try to catch it. The box hit me and fell to the pleather seat. I looked at the box and then at Mr. Chow in confusion.

"You clean yo-self up!" he barked.

Thanks for that Mr. Unprofessional. He walked out and I never saw him again. He did the exam, threw some Kleenex's at me from across the room, gave me orders and left me like a cheap whore. I was bewildered, but "I clean myself up" and walked to the front desk to the same smiling nurse. She said I was good to go and I tried my best to normally walk out of the door. I got in my car and just sat there for a second while listening to some sappy song on the radio as the cold rain fell. Did that just happen? Should I go home, run a hot shower and cry while in the fetal position? This was only the beginning of the end of my time in the service.

Drugs

Even though I was almost done being a soldier, I still had work to do with my Joes. They were coming back from war and needed mentoring or an occasional slap in the face.

"Tell me why you got arrested, Mitch," I ordered.

"Uhhh, I uh, crashed my car into a kids playground," Mitch responded.

"Any kids there?!"

"Naw, it was late."

"Were you drunk?"

"Naw, I did Spice. Funny thing is I thought I was going 35mph."

"Why is that funny?"

"Cops said I was doin' 10."

Mitch got off with a slap on the wrist, because there was no sign of alcohol or drugs in his blood. Spice was a substance a lot more potent than weed, but it wasn't testable in 2010. Eventually, testing could be done to detect it after several instances like this led to a long investigation of the substance that was easily attainable online.

I completely understand why the military needs to keep drugs away from soldiers; they operate killing machines. It wouldn't be a good idea to have a bunch of stoned or tweaked out, gun-toting crazies running around the battlefield. On the other hand, I don't have a problem with guys getting a quick escape if they don't have to do anything important for a while. Military life can take a toll on people and if drug use is done in a controlled environment where nobody gets hurt, I don't have a problem with it. As I was out-processing, I thought back to the more memorable moments where drugs played a role in my entertainment.

"Want some cookies, Vance? Hehehe," ODB asked from over the wooden wall between our bunks.

"What kind of cookies?" I enquired.

"Ohhh they're *SPECIAL* cookies my wife made."

"Hahaha! I'm good, man, but thanks!"

"They're sooooo good, heheheeeeee."

While at COP Cobra, ODB had his wife make cookies with some weed and then she sent them to Iraq. Probably the perfect remedy after a long day with some time off. ODB was an older guy that dealt with more joint pain than the rest of us. I absolutely approved of his medicinal cookie use. He'd giggle like a little kid until he passed out and got some good shuteye. ODB never hurt anyone or went running around naked while high. He just had a good laugh and went to sleep, forgetting about the shithole he was in and the fact that his family was on the other side of the world.

Cobra was where I happened to see the most drug use during my travels. Guys were going up on the roof of the barracks to smoke weed, guys would get whatever they could from local interpreters and steroids were beefing up a lot of guys.

Steroid use was absolutely hilarious to watch. A lot of small guys, like myself, were able to start tossing around large amounts of weight in a very short amount of time. They were all angrier than the average deployed soldier too. There was a 'health and welfare' search one day to find all the 'roids users. Since the commander that ordered the search was also 'juicing,' everyone got off easy. Steroids didn't appeal to me so I decided to partake in a different kind of substance.

"SGT Vance, you OK?" asked Carter.

"Yeah, man. I'm good," I replied

"Your lips are blue."

"I think I better lie down dennnnnn. Erydings spinnnnning."

About an hour and a half earlier I was in my drug consigliore's room. We affectionately called him Perma-Fried. He was a great guy with a fucked up past. We think his acid abuse as a civilian and the mystery pills his aunt sent in a Tylenol bottle led to his seizure towards the middle of my second deployment. Drugs aside, he didn't take shit from anyone and always watched my back.

"Take just half of this pill," Perma-Fried advised.

"Why just half?" I questioned.

"I took a whole one and it messed me up."

"Fair enough, I just need something to mellow out and sleep."

"That'll definitely do it. Give it about 30 minutes to kick in."

An hour and a half goes by and I still feel nothing. I asked Perma-Fried about it and he said to trust him, so I did. About 15 more minutes pass and I find myself wandering between everyone's wooden cubicle rooms without really knowing how I got there when Carter walked up and talked to me about my blue lip phenomenon. I went back to my sleeping area, laid down as the ceiling started spinning and I broke out into a hot sweat. After about 5 minutes of freaking out, it was night nights for Vance. I woke up 12 hours later ready for an ultra marathon. I felt great, but I will never be doing whatever the hell that substance was again.

From the outside, I can see how you'd be surprised at how many folks in the military have done drugs. Would I declare it all as drug "abuse?" No, but I can't deny the ramped use of the stuff. It's easy to get away with and when it's expensive to run a urinalysis in a time when defense cuts were well underway, the military tended to not be able to keep up with catching users. At least 10% of our troop was to be tested at random on a weekly basis while in garrison and occasionally we'd do 100%. That weekly test rarely happened.

The Last Day

Between appointments with doctors, cleaning my gear to turn in and verbally smacking around soldiers that drove SUV's into playgrounds, I would swing by the troop offices and see if I was needed to help train the guys on anything. Most of the time I wouldn't be needed and just did whatever I wanted. That's a nice thing about getting out of the service. As your time dwindles, the more freedom you're given. I enjoyed most of that treatment, but there was one day that just got to me. It was my last day in the service and unless you're getting dishonorably discharged, you get an ETS award and your platoon does something nice for you. The award simply recognizes you're done with your service and usually your platoon is proud to send you off properly. When I first joined the unit and veterans were getting out, they were presented with a saber with a meaningful engraving and a chance to address the entire troop. I watched that tradition fade over my 6 years of service. I walked into White's platoon cage where JD and Shorts were sitting that very morning. I'll never forget everything that was said and done.

"The fuck are you doing here?" JD asked with a scowl.

"Yeah, you don't need to be here," Shorts added.

"Therrrrre's nothing I need to do today?" I hinted.

"No, you're all done," said JD with an arrogant smirk.

"Bye," added Shorts.

I took a pause to just look at them in disbelief.

"Roger."

The matter of the award wasn't a big concern. I knew the First Sergeant was going to throw a temper tantrum when he found out I left without being handed the ETS shit, as is the tradition regardless of your relationship with your chain of command. The part that bothered me was that there I was with my first line supervisor and the acting platoon sergeant after 6 years of honorable service and their last words were, "The fuck are you doing here?" They neglected to give a handshake, a slap on the back or even a "Thanks for serving."

I didn't even argue. I just "rogered up" and walked away as my soldiers saw me looking betrayed. Maybe it was a prank. I didn't get along with those two at all, but I never once disrespected them or failed to do what they asked of me. I knew my soldiers loved me as much as I loved them. Something wasn't right. I drove back to my apartment, started cooking lunch and cracked open a beer. After 3 beers my cell rang. It was the platoon cage.

"Hello?"

"You need to come back. First Sergeant is pissed you went home. He said you aren't out of the service yet," JD said.

"I'm wasted," I lied.

"You have to get your ETS award in person."

I just hung up on him so he could sweat it out while I took my time getting there. JD was so full of shit with the "award in person" nonsense. That stuff can be mailed. He didn't have the balls to tell the First Sergeant what happened in the office. I drove back to Fort Lewis smelling like alcohol and furiously walked thru the troop area and out front to formation. Some of my soldiers were telling me they asked higher why I was gone without any kind recognition of service. I've never encountered loyalty greater than that group of young men.

The Commander at the time said some cheesy words and poked

fun at the fact I was an E-5 for so long, not knowing I turned down my E-6 over 2 years earlier to be a team leader. The First Sergeant didn't say a damn thing and then the floor was mine. Thanks for that amazing introduction. Instead of giving the Half-Baked, "Fuck you, fuck you, you're cool, fuck you, I'm out" speech I set aside all personal feelings and spoke about what was really important.

"This day isn't about me, guys. I want to take this opportunity to do what not enough people are doing. I want to say thank you. You volunteered... during a time of war... to be in combat arms. Those three things prove that you have more guts than 99.99% of this great country and for as long as I live, I will fight for you to be recognized as such. It doesn't matter if it's next week or a decade from now; if any of you need anything at anytime, I'm here for you. You'll always have a warm bed, cold beer and a lot of beautiful women in Virginia waiting. Getting out has been the toughest decision of my life. Thank you, thank you, thank you. That's all I got."

There were some guys holding back tears. Two guys in particular had a look on their face that resembled guilt. Fuck you very much. Shorts even grabbed me to make sure I was given the respect of a "Goodbye Pink Belly." Everyone had a slap, they helped me up and I started walking to my car when shitheads like JD offered, "We gotta get a drink sometime." Yeah guy, I won't hold my breath waiting for your call. I left knowing I did the right thing and still made an impact on those that acted like they didn't care. It was definitely a good time to get out as the idealist view of brotherhood I held on to so stubbornly had apparently turned rotten.

I went back to the apartment and finished my case of beer. I called my sister and she was in near tears that I was treated like that on my last day, but my "Joes" still put up a fight for me. Those guys were the best. On Veterans Day of 2010 I was still in Tacoma and a couple of them, Hall and Rogers, took me to my favorite bar. It happened to be on the first floor of my apartment complex. My sister, Heather, called the bartender and told him to put the drinks on her credit card. Up until then, it was the only time in my life I was surprised with such company and it felt great. The three of us ran up a decent tab and slammed glasses honoring our brethren and each other thru the night.

A few months later, when it was time for me to leave Tacoma for Virginia, I notified all the good soldiers that kept up with me that I would be at my favorite bar, The Imbibery, now Tacoma Cabana, on my last night in Washington. It was such an epic night. I found out the next week that a certain click in the platoon was offended they weren't invited. The most hysterical, yet sad, part of leaving the military was the perception people had of themselves in my own eyes. I was around for 6 more months and how many calls did I get from my former chain of command? Zero. I merely surrounded myself with good people my last night and anyone was welcome to join. I miss that bunch that showed up everyday of my life.

After a few more months, a certain military magazine printed an article titled, "All the Good NCO's are Gone."

P. T. S. Don't be a Douche Bag

"Why did you show up late and stoned for duty?" asked the First Sergeant.

"I have P.T.S.D. First Sergeant," Pudge replied.

"Well welcome to the fuckin' party! Everyone in this building has P.T.S.D. and you don't see us getting high or showing up whenever we want to!"

Touché, First Sergeant.... Tooooooouché.

P.T.S.D. is a sensitive subject for thousands of combat veterans. After my first tour of 15 months, we were all evaluated and most of us lied about how we felt, including myself. At the time we thought talking about the situations we were in was a sign of weakness. Then things started happening. After my second deployment I started making it a point to encourage guys not to lie when they were evaluated and be as honest as possible, especially since the meetings were confidential and not going on their permanent records.

I never thought I had any issues and felt confident that I could handle any situation with ease. After being evaluated back when I was out-processing the military to the joys of civilian life, I was humbled. Typically you talk for about 5 minutes with a military doctor and they check a bunch of boxes nobody cares about and off you go. When you transition to the civilian world, you talk to a civilian doctor. This lady got me good.

After 2 hours of her digging as deep into my mind as she could go, we were both in tears. I remember thinking, "What the hell just happened in here?" I felt Jedi-mind tricked into talking about my feelings and shit. Jedi-mind tricked by DS Anderson on the way in with bending metal and now by the doctor lady in the end. I told her this and we laughed. And you know what? It felt great. After that day I was an open book to who ever wanted to know anything about my adventures. I wouldn't start off any conversation with "Hey, so this one time, in Iraq, I stuck a flute...." You get the picture. I usually only talk about military stuff when people ask, but I'll occasionally initiate a conversation if I have a funny story. Anybody can relate to funny stories, right?

Even though I fought it and disagreed with her, she diagnosed me with P.T.S.D. It's strange to me to be "diagnosed" with something like that. I never saw my experiences as having a negative effect and that's how people unfortunately viewed P.T.S.D. at the time. I actually felt more comfortable and alive during a firefight than I did in a room full of familiar faces at my own house party... wait a minute... yep, that's probably not normal. That's the mentality of a lot of combatants though. It's a sense of detachment from what's normal that we all lack. I didn't figure it out until that doctor lady told me, and yes, I like saying the name "doctor lady" like a Neanderthal. After all kinds of evaluations, off I went to the naïve world of civilian life. Nobody noticed anything different about me, but sometimes I couldn't help myself. Every time the national anthem plays to this day... waterworks.

"Mat, are you OK?" a civilian friend would ask.

"Yeah, fuck off, I'm good," I'd reply as we both laughed.

I started going out to bars and focused on conversations not dealing with the military in fear of boring a local. Then I found that it wasn't easy at first, as I really didn't have much in common with anybody outside of my platoon. I'd see so many guys fail at sparking a conversation with a hippy chick they wanted to get digits from. There's nothing worse than a guy trying to get free drinks or a girl's number by volunteering "war stories." News flash gentlemen; when you're out in public and everyone is having a good time, NOBODY CARES ABOUT YOUR PAST. People just want to relax and have fun. If they ask, then that's their problem. Otherwise, chill out and enjoy the company.

In late February of 2011, I left Tacoma for my home in Alexandria, Virginia. I was excited for a fresh start in a place where people didn't judge you by how you "got your hair did." I started working at a local bar serving tables for extra cash and to pass the time with entertaining characters. One such character sat at the bar on most nights and drank until he got this creepy look in his eyes. That's when I knew he was about to inappropriately hit on a woman.

He claimed to be a veteran that thought his sob stories would get him laid. Pathetic. I never saw him succeed, yet on and on he went every night. Sometimes I would get behind the bar just to hear his latest lies. He would look at me as I passed by, having no idea I knew he was a lying sack of shit.

"It's tough, ya know? No, you sure wouldn't know. You gotta be a man like me to serve," he said often.

"Yes, sir. I could never be a man like you," I humbly replied.

People ask why I didn't call him out. The simple answer is that I was at work, but since I usually do call people out when I'm off work, I just found this case kind of entertaining. How far could I go with pulling fake stories out of this guy before the girl next to him realized he was not telling the truth as I got him tongue-tied with questions on "how to be a man?"

I could go on for a while with these stories, but here's the bottom line; P.T.S.D. just means we've experienced something different and unnatural to the typical American environment. I heard a quote that best captures it, "It's the body's natural reaction to an unnatural event." You don't have to go war to have it. It could happen if you lose someone close to you, if you're in a horrific car accident, if you're involved in a drive by... anything traumatizing. For those reasons, it drives me up a wall when people use it as an excuse to act like an asshole. We're not the world's first traumatized group of people! It was a volunteer military during a time of war. What did you expect? No matter what the circumstance, find someone that has experienced what you have and vent. Don't be "that guy" at the bar. Life goes on so we better jump on that wave and enjoy the ride before it crashes onto shore.

Revolv-a-lution

Combat vets: Did we have more bad days than good? Of course! That's war. The world continues to revolve around the sun and we are but mere specks. That's not to say we should forget the bad days, as they have taught us many lessons, but for our own mental health and the sake of everyone around us, we need to share the good stories! We have to remember that the only people that will ever understand us are the ones that were there when things went bad. Nobody else cares. It's human nature.

I'm happy now as a civilian. I still fantasize about worst-case scenarios wherever I am, but ultimately I hope for peace. It's as silly of a dream as a Utopian society, but it's my dream. In the mean time, I focus on helping other people; whether it be combat veterans, cancer patients or a motor cyclist that hit the guardrail on the exit ramp. I'm always ready to jump in and help as the majority of Americans are.

Before the military and combat, I was unsure of myself. I've evolved into something different. That something is a lot loopier, but there is certainly never a dull moment in my life thanks to my experiences. I don't hesitate to try new things or travel or put myself out there to be humiliated in the name of chasing my dreams. I see the world differently. I yearn for a worthy revolution, but I never take the freedoms in the United States for granted, which many people do. The only difficulty I have now is not taking people too seriously when they think living in the US is hard. They just haven't explored the world outside of their bubble. Don't get me wrong, we have tons of room to improve upon, but we are far better off than any other place I've seen.

You've completed the short stories of my comical adventures in the military. Did you laugh? Did you cry? Were you at all inspired? All three are components of good stories in my opinion. My main objective was to just create smiles and bring joy out of some awful places I've been, so if you did anything besides chuckle then that is icing on the cake. I left out all the blood, guts and heroism I witnessed to give you stories not often told. As with the Warno! section you read at the beginning, these stories make up a miniscule percentage of the rest of the stories other combatants can share. Reach out and ask them to tell you a funny story about their brothers. It will surely make them smile. Thank you for reading and always feel free to reach out and share your thoughts of this work. Well, take the negative ones and shove them up your ass... I'm kidding! But seriously, right up your corn hole.